Jump!

Also by Simon May

Nietzsche's Ethics and His War on 'Morality'
Thinking Aloud: A Handbook of Aphorisms
Love: A History
Love: A New Understanding of an Ancient Emotion
The Power of Cute
How to Be a Refugee

EDITED BY SIMON MAY

Nietzsche on Freedom and Autonomy (*with Ken Games*)
Nietzsche's 'On the Genealogy of Morality':
A Critical Guide

Jump!

*A New Philosophy for
Conquering Procrastination*

SIMON MAY

LONDON

First published in Great Britain in 2025 by Basic Books UK
An imprint of John Murray Press

1

Copyright © Simon May 2025

The right of Simon May to be identified as the Author of the Work has been asserted by him in accordance with the Copyright, Designs and Patents Act 1988.

All rights reserved. No part of this publication may be reproduced, stored in a retrieval system, or transmitted, in any form or by any means without the prior written permission of the publisher, nor be otherwise circulated in any form of binding or cover other than that in which it is published and without a similar condition being imposed on the subsequent purchaser.

A CIP catalogue record for this title is available from the British Library

Hardback ISBN 978-1-399-80709-8
ebook ISBN 978-1-399-80711-1

Typeset in Janson Text by
Palimpsest Book Production Ltd, Falkirk, Stirlingshire

Printed and bound in Great Britain by Clays Ltd, Elcograf S.p.A.

John Murray policy is to use papers that are natural, renewable and recyclable products and made from wood grown in sustainable forests. The logging and manufacturing processes are expected to conform to the environmental regulations of the country of origin.

Carmelite House
50 Victoria Embankment
London EC4Y 0DZ

www.basicbooks.uk

John Murray Press, part of Hodder & Stoughton Limited
An Hachette UK company

The authorised representative in the EEA is
Hachette Ireland, 8 Castlecourt Centre,
Dublin 15, D15 XTP3, Ireland (email: info@hbgi.ie)

In grateful and loving memory of PMF,
who never procrastinated

Contents

PART I
Swerving Our Life

1. Putting Off Our Most Cherished Priorities — 3
2. The Cult of Work — 19
3. The Cult of Autonomy — 31

PART II
Seven Ways to Unleash Motivation

4. Lower the Stakes — 47
5. Remember We Are Mortal — 71
6. Embrace the Spirit of Play — 85
7. Harness the Power of Regret — 101
8. Let Boredom Save Us — 117
9. Resist the Mirage of Complete Fulfilment — 133
10. Cultivate Attentiveness — 153

Conclusion: When Procrastination Can Be a Blessing — 169

Acknowledgements — 183
Notes — 185
Index — 199

Procrastination is the thief of time;
Year after year it steals.
       Edward Young, *Night Thoughts*

I have wasted time, and now doth time waste me.
       Shakespeare, *Richard II*

Grant me chastity and continence, but not yet.
       Augustine, *Confessions*

PART I
Swerving Our Life

PART I

Severing Our Ties

I

Putting Off Our Most Cherished Priorities

Do you repeatedly defer life to later, convinced there will come a time when you'll be optimally prepared to seize its opportunities? Do you spend your best hours on chores or trivia before allowing yourself to get to what most matters to you? Do you avoid pursuing a treasured goal for the sake of an easier or more immediately pleasurable activity – although you believe that doing so will harm you?

Many of us procrastinators will unhesitatingly answer yes to these questions. We might recall, too, how we knowingly embarked on romantic relationships or even marriages with the wrong people all the while assuring ourselves that we'd eventually choose someone we genuinely love. Or how we postponed the vocation we craved and instead spent years in occupations alien to who we are. Or how we put off living more healthily, aware of the harm we'd likely inflict on ourselves by going on as we were.

As a result, we spend too much of our life mourning the time we've lost, the energy we've misspent, the chances we've missed out on that might never return. Perhaps the worst part of it is that we were sure of what we wanted all along, and yet we kept wilfully dodging it, consigning its pursuit to a nebulous future and submitting to the urge to do something else less arduous. Or to sabotage our own success and fulfilment. Or to avoid testing our abilities and finding them wanting.

All this can feel irrational. We're knowingly inflicting harm on ourselves, but we do it nonetheless – often under cover of the illusion, with which I'm all too familiar, that there's always more time in life to get around to our priorities; or that, after further delay, progress on them will somehow come more easily to us; or that another bout of relaxing distractions will boost our motivation to pursue them.

But there's one reassuring reality here: we're not lazy. The fact that we're so tortured by our stuckness and wasted time; that we turn again and again to the goals we most care about; that when we procrastinate over them we cast around for some productive or at least enjoyable displacement activity – all this is evidence that our problem isn't indolence. Rather, it's self-sabotaged motivation. It's that we avoid what we most value – what we most want to go after.

For indolence and laziness are states of inactivity in which action and intention are suspended, surrendered, or simply absent – states of 'Tumid apathy with no concentration', in T. S. Eliot's marvellous words.[1] By contrast, procrastinators can be stubbornly ambitious – knots of fierce intent.

And there's another key difference between indolence and procrastination. Indolence is often a lifestyle choice – and in some cultures, such as the ancient Roman, a proudly displayed privilege of an aristocratic elite, a mark of the leisure peculiar to a noble way of life. But I doubt anyone would regard procrastination as a lifestyle choice – as the prescription for the best life to lead; a symbol of status to which the less fortunate can only aspire.

Nor are we likely to find anything beautiful, or elegant, in procrastination in the way that we might in leisure or *dolce far niente* – the exquisite pleasure of lingering in the present; freely, indifferent to goals and their achievement, and with no care for our future well-being. On the contrary: we procrastinators are painfully aware of our goals and their non-achievement. And we care very much about our future well-being. We plan for it; we're anxious for how it might turn out; we pamper it with open-ended and often extravagant promises of getting around to doing what we need to flourish.

In the meantime, we won't do nothing. Rather we'll likely devote ourselves to a succession of substitute tasks that we might never have been motivated to pursue were they not in the service of escape from our priorities. I'm not referring only to binge online surfing, watching multiple news reports of the same event, cleaning the kitchen, or other activities that would otherwise be uninteresting or even oppressive. Although we usually think of displacement activities as trivial, they can be anything but. They can include the most demanding jobs and professions, serious romantic relationships, and long-term marriages. Yet for all the delight, fascination, and security they afford us, we find that we never love them – and even resent them, eventually saying to ourselves, with the apostle Paul, 'I do the very thing I hate'.[2]

In fact, some procrastinators pursue a substitute activity with such alacrity and brilliance and diligence that neither the people who applaud them nor even they themselves (for some of the time) are conscious that they're motivated by a deep urge to escape what they most care about. Their achievements in this activity might be the lifetime ambition of others, commanding the widest admiration.

Such triumphant procrastination can take over our life, so that we spend years swerving priorities that are key to who we take ourselves to be and want to become. The romance for which we've been yearning but repeatedly failed to pursue when we had the chance. The vocation on which we've set our heart, but set to one side 'for the time being' while we take a series of jobs that we know in advance won't truly fulfil us. The move to another city or country that we long to make but endlessly put off. The bucolic life of which we dream, but avoid by frenetic activity. A successful substitute life can also be a form of procrastination – indeed one of its most powerful forms, hiding itself in plain sight. We become trapped in it precisely by our effectiveness at it.

My mother had a friend who studied pottery, her first and deepest calling, but then became a plastic surgeon, tempted by the money, the glamour, and a well-established professional ladder, each rung of which would guarantee further status – sources of robust security almost unknown to the lone potter. The plan was to do this for twenty years, as a preparatory life to her real one, after which, she promised herself, she would return to pottery, hopefully fortified by success.

The plan worked superbly. She became a top authority in her field, director of one of her country's university hospitals, and a recipient of high honours – all the while taking herself to be temporarily deferring her true vocation.

Loyal to her commitment, she didn't defer it for ever. Upon her retirement, half a century after first studying pottery, she returned to it, sitting once more in a classroom with eighteen-year-olds, and went on to have a deeply fulfilled old age – yet one suffused by regret that she would no longer have time to develop her full potential as a potter.

A highly remunerated lawyer I once met – who'd hankered to become an artist since early youth and knew exactly what kind of art he wanted to make – finally gave up his partnership in a prestigious law firm in his forties, shocked into action by the onset of middle age and the accelerating passage of time. Guided by a meticulous strategy that he applied to everything he cared about, each step mapped out together with the time he would devote to it, he spent four years at art school during which time his own style became excitingly apparent to him; he rented the perfect studio; he determined what works he would start on after he'd fitted out his studio with the best lighting, materials, and equipment that money could buy; and he forged wide contacts in the art world among critics, gallerists, and fellow artists. Yet, he never took the step all this activity was preparing him for; he never began to make art. *That* was always around the corner.

What do the surgeon and the lawyer, who both reached the summit of their temporary profession, show? They remind us that displacement activities can be so rewarding in terms of fulfilment, prestige, and financial security that, despite leaving us with the gnawing pain of living estranged from who we take ourselves to really be, we might persist with them for decades, long after they've yielded their plentiful rewards. They show us that procrastination can have style.

Not that it always involves displacement activity. When, in his *Confessions*, the great Christian philosopher Augustine (354–430 CE) recalls his youthful prayer asking God to grant him 'chastity and continence [i.e. self-control], but not yet',[3] the weakness of will that he rues isn't that he pursued sensual pleasures merely as a diversion from the demanding self-rule needed for a life of devotion to God. The whole point was that he had indulged in 'lust' for its own sake, on account of the intense delight it afforded him. As he candidly admits, he 'preferred to satisfy rather than suppress' it – and certainly 'preferred it to the alternatives', above all to following God. Indeed, addressing God, he acknowledges that he was 'afraid you might hear my prayer quickly, and that you might too rapidly heal me of the disease of lust'.

Here's one of procrastination's devilish tricks, one of its crucial enablers: it makes us believe that the deferral is always temporary; that, in the long term, we'll lose nothing decisive by it. The road not travelled is still open, we tell ourselves; whatever we're postponing remains for the taking. Just as for Augustine there was always another tomorrow to which he could postpone the life change that he yearned to make at some point and for which he repeatedly prayed: to abandon sexual indulgence for chastity and self-control. Which was hardly any life change since it was central to achieving what he took to be his supreme goal: to lead a genuinely Christian life. But, he appears to have convinced himself, the cost of deferment, though real, was affordable. Whether he pursued it tomorrow or the day after would make no appreciable difference.

None of these procrastinators – the surgeon belatedly turned potter, the wannabe artist, Augustine with his 'not yet' – would have been helped by the familiar recommendations to be found in so many works on overcoming procrastination. They wouldn't have pursued their real callings by focusing on a single big project at any one time and deciding in advance 'what to fail at', as Oliver Burkeman proposes in a fascinating book subtitled *Time Management for Mortals*.[4]

Nor would they have found the solution in Cal Newport's advice in *Slow Productivity*,[5] which boils down to 'doing fewer things, working at a natural pace, and obsessing over quality'. Nor, too, in all probability, in breaking up the task of achieving each priority into bite-sized steps, imposing a deadline on every step, working on it for no more than twenty-five minutes at a time followed by short relaxation breaks (the so-called Pomodoro® Technique), keeping to-do lists updated daily, carving out enough leisure time – and then just doing it!

For all three of my procrastinators *did know* what their top life priorities were – in fact, they had crystal-clear priorities to which they never ceased to be devoted. (That's the whole point of the kind of procrastination that sabotages a flourishing life: it swerves what the procrastinator craves, steering a wide berth around precisely the person they want to be – often when they're convinced that doing so will prevent them leading their best life.) Moreover, the hugely successful plastic surgeon and the high-flying lawyer explicitly focused on one big project or priority at a time. They were quite obviously obsessive when it came to quality, without, it seems, being paralysed by perfectionism. And they had a strategy to eventually pursue their dreams, comprising discrete tasks backed up by to-do lists, deadlines, and exemplary time management. Yet they still deferred those dreams.

By contrast, conventional solutions to procrastination work best for tasks we've got to do but which aren't already cherished priorities – and where the problem is *low motivation*, not sabotaged motivation. In particular, they're good for inspiring progress in a dull or alienating job; for chores like filing taxes, getting that gas safety check, or cleaning up the office. These are tasks that make us feel like we're administering life rather than living it, and for which we have little or no enthusiasm in the first place. We often lack impetus to pursue them until their neglect begins to seriously endanger us, or – ironically – they can be pressed into service as displacement activity from our real priorities. In such cases setting limited priorities and improving time management – working 'smarter not harder' in the jargon – will succeed best.

There are, however, many other reasons why we procrastinate, some of them more fundamental than a lack of well-ordered priorities or inadequate time management. Their sheer number can be baffling, and each of us will need to decide which are at work in our own case. Sometimes the reason is precisely the importance to us of a treasured priority – its intimidatingly high stakes and demanding nature – as with the aspiring artist and potter. Or, because it's crucial to us, we set such exalted standards for achieving it that we fear or know in advance we won't be able to meet them, and so we procrastinate to avoid the letdown and the humiliation. Or we overburden our priority with securing self-esteem and the esteem of others. Or we pursue it at the wrong time in life – before we're emotionally ready or have the necessary skills and clarity of purpose. Or we fear that our priority might prove empty in the end, failing to provide the deep satisfaction we hope to find in it – so that it's best left unattained, shrouded in alluring mystery.[6] Or perhaps we fear that *all* demanding goals will fail to provide stable fulfilment; that however much we achieve we'll always end up feeling somehow empty. Or, more mysteriously, we flee it to avoid the joy and fulfilment in pursuing what we really want to do. Or, equally mysteriously, we dread that choosing and pursuing a deeply loved priority – a choice that necessarily also closes off other choices – will, bizarre though it might seem, somehow bring to heightened awareness the reality that we, like everyone, are set on an irreversible trajectory towards death, the ultimate signature of life's transience. Or, more generally, we are fatally demotivated by the thought that death will render all our striving pointless. Or we somehow dread self-definition – retreating before the strange terror of becoming real to ourselves – and so we flee from becoming who we really are. Or, finally, we lack the attentiveness that's needed to persist with any demanding task.

In Part II, I'll explore these reasons to procrastinate and propose how they can each be overcome. Suffice it to say now that any solution to them must tackle head on the fear by which they're fuelled, so as to rescue our innate motivation to pursue what we most care about. For nothing decapitates the will like fear. Whether it's fear of failure or fear of success. Indeed, one reason why a displacement activity can be so compelling is precisely because it's relatively free of such sources of fear and perceived risk – and because it might also offer the quickest path to self-esteem, social status, power, and a life of comfort – as was the case for the lawyer and the surgeon.

To sum up, the key question on which I'm focusing is how to overcome procrastination over our top life priorities. Over those goals that we take to define who we are and want to become: goals that promise to fill our lives with purpose and meaning and joy. Goals that seem built into us by all the force that nature and life experience can muster. Goals that we're often brimming with desire to achieve.

For this most distressing procrastination – avoiding, resisting, even sabotaging what we passionately crave to do and the life we ardently hope to live – I'll argue that we need a very different approach than those of conventional solutions, one that releases motivation from the clutches of fear, of dull routine, and of perspectives that paralyse action. In doing so, I will turn for occasional insights to the long history of alarm about why we knowingly swerve what we take to be in our best interests. It's a history that goes back to the earliest recorded times: 'Friend, stop putting off work and allow us to go home in good time', reads an Egyptian hieroglyphic dating from 1400 BCE. 'Do not put off your work till tomorrow and the day after; for a sluggish worker does not fill his barn', the Greek poet Hesiod warns in his epic poem *Works and Days*, written around 800 BCE.[7] Most of my historical examples will, though, be drawn from later thinkers: from Plato and Aristotle in ancient Greece of the fifth and fourth centuries BCE to the desert monks of fourth century CE Egypt; from the thirteenth-century medieval Christian theologian Thomas Aquinas to the sixteenth-century religious reformer Martin Luther and the eighteenth-century wit and polymath Samuel Johnson. Although the English word 'procrastination' is of relatively recent coinage – dating from the sixteenth century – the question of why we might defer our supreme ends, despite believing this will be bad for us, has puzzled people for millennia, evoking very different explanations of what causes it and how it can be overcome.

Very broadly, such historical explanations fall into two distinct camps, or at least camps with distinct emphases. They diagnose what we today call procrastination as predominantly an ethical failing or else as predominantly a medical/organic problem. On the ethical diagnosis, which will be my principal focus, procrastination centrally occasions self-blame, regret, and culpable boredom with how we're leading our life – a clear sense of moral failure for not living it as we should and could, and so of dereliction of our duties and responsibilities to ourselves and others. On a medical or biological understanding, by contrast, it's usually less overtly blameworthy and more the result of a particular constitution of our bodies, minds, or souls, or of adverse experiences we've endured – some, at least, of which are taken to lie beyond our responsibility and control. Not surprisingly, within each camp procrastination has been framed in diverse ways according to the particular background picture of human willing that's at work.

As an ethical failing it's been conceptualized by Greek philosophers like Plato and Aristotle as weakness of will that causes us to act against our best judgement of what's good for us. Here, as Plato understands it, the capacity that's deemed to be lacking is *reason*, which if it worked properly would make it impossible to pursue a course of action that we know and believe isn't, all things considered, in our best interests.

For an influential strand of the Christian tradition, exemplified by the towering twelfth-century philosopher Thomas Aquinas, the malaise is an oppressive and sinful *sorrow* which turns us away from God – our highest possible spiritual good. And which induces a lovelessness, expressed in mental torpor, so pervasive that we abandon all striving for what we know is the best way to live our life.

For other schools of thought still, the failing at the heart of procrastination is *impatience* that causes us to choose an immediate reward over a later reward, even if the later one is substantially larger. Differently put, it's excessive devotion to easy pleasures which motivates us to defer priorities costing effort and pain.

In the modern period, since faith in a saving God began to wane in the eighteenth century, the relevant deficiency has sometimes been diagnosed as a short-sighted failure to appreciate the brevity of our transient life, often accompanied by faith in an eternal post-mortem existence whose effortless and undistracted blessings will vastly outweigh any deficiencies in our earthly accomplishments. Such failure might be expressed as a refusal, complacent or defiant, to recognize that we have one shot at living this life – our only life – well, and that we can never know when we will run out of time and opportunity to make a go of it.

As a medical or organic problem, however, procrastination has been understood in a significantly different way: as listlessness or melancholy rooted in malfunctions, predispositions, or impairments of our organism. This kind of diagnosis is found in, for example, Hindu, Greek, and Roman theories of the 'humours', which are of three or four basic kinds, the relative proportions of which are taken to govern health and sickness. Remarkably, such explanations of procrastination – which I won't have space to consider in this book – endured in the West for more than two millennia, from ancient times right up to the nineteenth century.[8]

In a Hindu medical text such as the *Charaka Samhita*, which was composed sometime between 100 BCE and 100 CE, the diagnosis would be an excess of the humour associated with torpor or inertia (*tamas*) over the other two – lucidity or light (*sattva*) and energy or passion (*rajas*).[9] In the Greek tradition, originating in the fifth century BCE with Hippocrates (460–c. 375) and formalized in the second century CE by the philosopher and doctor Galen (129–c. 216) – and so in remarkable parallel with the Hindu system – what we today call procrastination would be diagnosed as an excess of black bile over the three other humours – yellow bile, blood, and phlegm. Each of these humours is correlated to a particular temperament or mood using terms that we continue to employ today: yellow bile predisposes to a 'choleric' temperament; blood to a 'sanguine' disposition; black bile to 'melancholia'; and phlegm to a 'phlegmatic' character. Dominance of melancholia would be confirmed if you exhibited symptoms such as restlessness, inability to concentrate, and a propensity to keep switching tasks as each one, in turn, gets on your nerves and you seek escape into yet another.

Other historical explanations have included astrological doctrines, prominent in the Italian Renaissance of the fourteenth to sixteenth centuries, claiming that the relative positions of the planets, especially at one's birth, shape one's energy levels, talents, and sundry internal determinants of one's life and fate. In particular, people born under the sign of Saturn will be prone to torpor, fatigue, and gloom – marks of what is still called the 'saturnine' temperament.[10]

Since the nineteenth century in Europe, the rise of the psychological sciences, including psychoanalysis, has generated a variety of explanations – for example, in terms of depression or anxiety resulting from adverse childhood experiences, such as abuse, failures to be loved or recognized, and loss of a real or ideal object of love. Such explanations, which I will only touch on, have been joined by diagnoses of attention deficit disorders (ADD, ADHD), chronic fatigue immune dysfunction syndrome, myalgic encephalomyelitis (ME), cognitive bias that imagines tasks to be less arduous if performed in the future than if undertaken now, and the related idea, associated with the behavioural economist George Ainslie, that our impulses seek smaller rewards sooner over larger rewards later. Meanwhile neuroscience has framed the problem as an imbalance or contest between parts of the brain, notably between the impulsive, pleasure-seeking limbic system and the planning, calculating prefrontal cortex, and/or as resulting from deficiencies of neurotransmitters such as serotonin.

These are only part of a rich field of biological or medical explanations, but they have one feature in common: even if they hold that procrastination can be aggravated by lifestyle or mindset – for example, poor diet or posture, excessive mental or physical exertion, stressful job choices, or pervasive worry – which are taken to be within an individual's control, they are less strikingly freighted with attributions of blame, guilt, and responsibility than are those that fall squarely within the ethical category.

Both the ethical and the medical/biological understandings of procrastination extend back far before the early modern era in the West, which burst into life in the sixteenth century. Since then, however, two further and unprecedented sources of it have appeared, which, because of the extremes to which they've been taken in our time, have given an entirely novel twist to this ancient problem of knowingly acting against our better judgement. They are the twin ideals – more than ideals, cults – of autonomy and work. And they, more than any other development – and certainly more than the new universe of distraction opened up by personal electronic devices and online media – explain why we are living today in a golden age of the procrastinator. It is to them that we should now turn.

2
The Cult of Work

How could the cult of work have come to foster procrastination? Wouldn't this be a contradiction in terms? Surely the value we place on work is crucial to *overcoming* any impulse to procrastinate over it? Surely it's key to giving purpose and dignity to our lives; vital to expressing who we take ourselves to be, including our talent, our drive, and our ingenuity; a way of leaving our mark upon the world; and, to that extent, fundamental to establishing our worth and distinctiveness both in our own eyes and those of our peers?

On the one hand, the cult of work is certainly all of these things. It has also unleashed extraordinary inventiveness, underwritten vast increases in freedom and opportunity, and enabled prodigious self-discovery and self-creation. It has been central to the explosion of sciences and the arts, productivity and technology in the past two hundred years. And it continues to be so.

On the other hand, the cult of work as it has widely developed in Western industrialized countries has turned many of us into robotic productivity machines, slaves to the deity of relentless output. Our identities have become dependent on an unceasing stream of achievements and our self-esteem, along with others' esteem for us, poised perilously atop our CVs.

The result can be to deeply alienate us from our work – not only when we're indentured to an impersonal bureaucratic organization run by remote bosses or stakeholders, but even when we're pursuing work that we freely choose, in control of its aims and schedules, and able to reap its fruits. For the way the cult of work has developed has turned our lives into a kind of industrial process – replete with targets, deadlines, and deliverables – to be managed with the maximum efficiency of a production line. In doing so, work easily goes from being a source of dignity to the very opposite, a source of self-alienation that demoralizes and paralyses us.

It's perhaps no coincidence that the English word 'procrastination', derived from the Latin for 'putting off until tomorrow', first appears in the sixteenth century when the earliest shoots of the cult of work emerge.[1] Since then it's been freighted with ever more moral opprobrium, and has come to exact a peculiar sort of emotional torture in a culture, like many in the West, that prizes work as a supreme good and so as a fundamental determinant of who we've become and how well we're living our lives. For those cultures, perhaps to a greater extent than ever before, we *are* our work.

Numerous opinion surveys bear this out. In a report of January 2019, the Pew Research Center found that over 90 per cent of teens, asked about their priorities for adult life, ranked 'having a job or career they enjoy' as 'extremely or very important' – and higher than any other priority, including 'helping other people who are in need' (81 per cent), having a lot of money (51 per cent), getting married (47 per cent), having children (39 per cent), or – perhaps surprisingly – becoming famous (11 per cent). As another

Pew Report, of January 2023, suggests, this seems to reflect the priorities imparted to them by their parents, of whom around 90 per cent rated financial independence and enjoyable careers or jobs as 'extremely or very important' for their children's future, while only about 20 per cent attached similar importance to their children becoming parents and getting married.[2]

Nor, crucially, does the ethos of work stop at vocations, careers, and jobs. This is only its most obvious manifestation. Much more surreptitiously, it has come to colonize *almost everything* we value, including relationships, religion, raising children, and keeping our homes, all of which have come to be seen or spoken of as work. I'm not making the familiar point that online connectivity and remote work have bulldozed the walls between public and private, work and 'life', so that we're always available to our careers or jobs. I mean that the ethos of work itself has come to penetrate everything we do, including what we've successfully carved out as private and intimate. We talk of 'working at love', 'working at our marriage', 'working on myself' – or, even, more colloquially, to a server in a restaurant enquiring if they can clear our plate, 'I'm still working on it'. Leisure, too, has become a kind of work – a time to be used productively and often to recharge ourselves to return, all the more energetically, to our jobs. Our life itself is understood as a 'work in progress'.

In other words, the point is not just that work in the sense of a job or a career has become a kind of religious cult. A cult that, as a determinant of social status (perhaps especially for highly educated elites), widely trumps even the value attached to success in love, parenting, and family. It's also that the cult of work no longer stops at career and its fruits, such as the satisfactions of achievement, status, and money. Rather its ethos permeates nearly every other dimension of life. Life has, in many ways, become a totalitarianism of work.[3]

This co-opting of life's goals, great and small, into serving the cult of work is now so ingrained that it seems self-evident. But merely to conjure with, say, a few of the great romances and marriages of history is to realize how peculiar it is to our age. It would be bizarre to imagine that Paris and Helen, as Homer's *Iliad* describes their passion, saw themselves as working on their relationship – or, for that matter, Eloise and Abelard, Shah Jahan and Mumtaz Mahal, Queen Victoria and Prince Albert, or Gertrude Stein and Alice B. Toklas. In reflecting on their relationships, these couples might have seen, for example, listening, attending, compromising, self-giving, and patience as virtues essential to the development of their love – virtues that must be cultivated through practice. But the contemporary idiom of work is pervaded by something quite distinct from these virtues – something that has come to govern how we pursue them today: namely, a spirit, redolent of industry and commerce, of productivity, of process, of bankable accomplishments, of time as a commodity, of programmes and projects. In short, of managerialism.

In this world of total work our self-worth equals our roster of achievements. A romance is an achievement. Leisure activities are an achievement. Our identity is an achievement. Even having children is spoken of as an achievement. In a related spirit, parenting is experienced as a form of engineering – designed both to maximize the autonomy of one's kids in constructing their own identities and to foster their peak performance in as many fields, curricular and extracurricular, as they can pack into their schedule. I have lost count of how many middle-class parents I've met who are so exhausted by what they describe as the 'relentlessness' of a weekend's domestic programme – in which everything their children do, from homework to sports to resolving quarrels, needs to be supervised, aided, and often attended – that they look forward to a busy working week in the office as a break. Their children, in turn, are inculcated with an ideal of life defined by an unceasing treadmill of goals, choices, competitive achievements, and CV building, from earliest schooling through every stage of education, towards the top universities, resulting in a well-paying and status-rich career ladder.

In the cult-like devotion it engenders, this ethos of work is not just religious in spirit but religious in origin. It can be traced back to that wellspring of the modern West, the Protestant Reformation of the sixteenth and seventeenth centuries, and in particular to two of its most important leaders, Martin Luther (1483–1546) and John Calvin (1509–64). Here is born the conviction – the moral conviction – that dedication to work, and success in work, are marks of righteousness, and so are necessarily deserved, while failure betrays moral laxity and is the just desert for a life of slacking.[4]

For Luther and Calvin, inactivity was a sure augur of perdition. Through them work was elevated to 'godly' status – not just the labour of a select few, such as a monk's life of contemplation and self-sufficiency had already been for centuries, but any honest toil. Whether humble or exalted, whether it issued in riches or merely in subsistence, work was a service to God – a form of devotion to the source of all goodness.

Remarkably, their exaltation of work – and of such virtues conducive to work as diligence and frugality – occurred despite the fact that Luther and, even more so, Calvin insisted that it couldn't influence whether God would elect to save or damn people. To imagine that it could do so was like saying that God could be persuaded or bribed to act as mere mortals wished. Which was not merely presumptuous but blasphemous. And, in any case, useless; for, Calvin insists, even before we're born, God has decided whether our fate is eternal salvation or eternal damnation. The die has already been cast, and nothing we do will change what is predestined.

Nonetheless, for both these Protestant leaders, although our works cannot *influence* the fate that God has already chosen for us, they can *reflect* it.[5] Diligence in work is, to that extent, a sign that we might be among the blessed. Whereas idleness points to damnation; it's one of the vices that Calvin banned from the city-state of Geneva when he became its religious dictator in 1555. To avoid one's allotted labour – to be what today is called a shirker – wasn't only to betray one's community; it portended the fires of hell.

This reification of work was continued by a long succession of religious preachers, such as the great eighteenth-century Puritan theologian, Jonathan Edwards (1703–58), who fulminated that people were avoiding the only goal that ultimately mattered – the pursuit of divine redemption – through distraction by ordinary pleasures and pastimes. They were wasting time with a lavish abandon that they would never risk even with their money, and postponing what really mattered:

To how little good purpose do many spend their time. There is nothing more precious, and yet nothing that men are more wasteful of . . . Mankind acts as if time was a thing that they had in greatest plenty, and as if they had a great deal more than they needed, and knew not what to do with it.[6]

At around the same time, polymath Samuel Johnson (1709–84) devoted one whole essay of his periodical *The Rambler* to lamenting the perils of procrastination. 'The folly', Dr Johnson remarked, 'of allowing ourselves to delay what we know cannot be finally escaped is one of the general weaknesses, which, in spite of the instruction of moralists, and the remonstrances of reason, prevail to a greater or lesser degree in every mind'. And, he continued, 'even they who most steadily withstand [such delay], find it, if not the most violent, the most pertinacious of their passions, always renewing its attacks, and, though often vanquished, never destroyed'.[7]

Johnson's diagnosis of procrastination is subtler than that of a firebrand like Edwards. It can be so intractable, he says, because it hasn't just one type of cause – say, hedonistic distractions – but many. For example, we are poor at deciding between rival desires, which allows those that are currently the loudest to take charge. We tend to get so bogged down in weighing up the pros and cons of different options that chance ends up choosing for us. And fear of the hardships that a particular course of action might involve can magnify them to the point of paralysis.

Johnson is no theologian. But his insistence that any moments which we cannot 'resolve to make useful by devoting them to the great business of [our] being' will inevitably be 'usurped by powers' beyond our control issues from the same Protestant tradition forged two centuries earlier by the leaders of the Reformation. It's a tradition that reaches its devotional apogee in such nineteenth-century writers as Thomas Carlyle (1795–1881), for whom work becomes, quite explicitly, 'religious', 'sacred', and our 'life purpose'. 'A man perfects himself by working,' Carlyle writes, for work is a 'purifying fire'.[8]

It's intrinsic to anything deemed sacred that its value is indisputable – and no longer a matter of preference or practicality, however convincing. Moreover, sacredness is generally a status assigned by the community. And, as early sociologists like Émile Durkheim (1858–1917) had already argued, what a community considers sacred is a key source of its collective identity and morality. So if work came to be experienced as a sacred life purpose in Johnson's and Carlyle's times, it's hardly surprising that since then it has increasingly colonized people's lives until, as I suggested just now, everything is thought of as work – and so needs to be 'worked at': love, sex, marriage, parenting, homemaking, friendships, even leisure. Nor therefore is it surprising that all these aspects of life become seen as labour that issues in productive achievements, measured by goals, milestones, and attainments. Or that all become infused with a potent combination of moralism and managerialism – moralism because work is seen as a virtue that lends righteousness and validity to our ends in life; managerialism because those ends are pursued in a process-driven spirit of targets, planning, execution, and completion. Even experience comes to be understood in this way: as an output of our life; an attainment that we've clocked up; a taking possession of the world to be maximized in quantity and quality. So that the sum of our experiences measures how productively and therefore how fully we're living.

When it comes to the cult of work, then, we're all lifers. Shortening the working week, making its hours more flexible, and ensuring its key decisions are more inclusive of workers and other stakeholders, greatly desirable though they are in themselves, will not change the reality that work is the most resilient of modern totalitarian ideologies. To see ourselves – and to be deemed by our peers – as leading a meaningful life crucially depends on our pursuing a full roster of activities whose value is measured by their total productivity or experiences or both. No dimensions of life are insulated from the spirit of work, as the mantra of the 'work–life balance' seems to imply.

Which brings us back to the opening question of this chapter: how could the cult of work have – paradoxically – come to foster procrastination? I think the answer is that when it degenerates into an ethos of productivity ruled by the spirit of managerialism, and when this ethos comes to imbue not just our jobs but so much of our life – career, marriage, raising kids, leisure – it can easily become uninspired, formulaic, stale, and limiting, even if we've chosen to pursue all of these ends freely and even if we're highly successful at them. Framing everything in the idiom of work can maroon us on a Sisyphean treadmill where we are little more than the sum of our achievements, recognition of which is perilously transient and readily swamped by the larger or more recent achievements of others.

Addicted to this ethos, and further yoked to it by social expectations, we feel like cogs in our own productivity machine – our energies, our minds, our resilience, our life itself experienced as assets geared towards maximizing our output. In this manner of relating to ourselves, work becomes addictive because it is so crucial to purpose, to self-respect, to social status, to control over our life and our world, and even to our sense of our own reality. Yet, it also becomes coldly unfulfilling, even when we excel at it. It becomes an inner tyrant that rules our life, giving a meaning to its many dimensions, far beyond career and vocation, while it also leaves us feeling strangely empty, devoid of relatedness, of play, of joy. Because we have become colonized by the ethos of work, we cannot let it go. So we keep at it, but then find we lack the morale to make progress with the task in hand. In short, we procrastinate.

Being motivated by high ideals isn't enough to rescue us from this ethos. We might, say, be committed to our vocation for the benefit of our community and perform our duties to our spouse and children under the star of love, but the routines by which we pursue even those commitments in practice (and practice is what dominates our everyday life) can still be suffused with the desiccating, process-driven managerialism of targets, planning, execution, and completion.

3
The Cult of Autonomy

Enter the other great cult of modernity: the astonishingly radical promise of individual autonomy. Repudiating millennia of tradition, it insists that our ends in life should not be given to us by any external authorities, be they priests, parents, peers, convention, rulers, holy texts, or a god or gods. Rather, what we value, achieve, think, and do should be imposed or endorsed by our own inner authority – whether that authority is understood as reason, as feeling, as will, as our nature, or otherwise as who we are or take ourselves to be. Once we have sovereignly decided what we ought to be and do, then we can – should – just be and do it.

By far the most influential and systematic source of this promise was the eighteenth-century philosopher Immanuel Kant (1724–1804) – although his thinking in turn has deep roots in the sixteenth and seventeenth centuries, epitomized by such giants as Martin Luther and René Descartes (1596–1650). Kant argued that only we, as individual rational subjects, can give ourselves the moral law by which our action is to be guided. Only individuals can originate and legitimate genuinely moral ends. We should never accept values simply on external authority. This goes equally for the most devout believers, who must autonomously endorse divine commandments if these are to be morally binding on them.[1] Which leads Kant to the extraordinary conclusion that in genuinely willing the highest moral good human beings are 'analogous to the divinity'.[2] In his vision of autonomy as legislating our own ends, Kant – outrageously to his contemporaries and perhaps even to our time – puts each of us on a footing with God. Indeed, in giving the moral law to ourselves, we supersede the authority of God. There is a direct line from him to the nineteenth-century philosophical firebrand Friedrich Nietzsche (1844–1900), perhaps the greatest spokesperson and prophet of the modern age, with his challenge to create one's own values and to supervise their implementation as demandingly as the old God would create and supervise divinely ordained values:

> Can you give yourself your own evil and your own good and hang your own will over yourself as a law? Can you be your own judge and avenger of your law? Terrible it is to be alone with the judge and avenger of one's own law. Thus is a star thrown out into the void and into the icy breath of solitude.[3]

Out of this heady mix – where the individual is gloriously self-determining, but at the price of 'the icy breath of solitude' – has sprung the modern Western promise of command and control over ever more areas of human life – and of the natural world around us too. Under its sway, one sphere after another of what was, since time immemorial, regarded as given – by the divine, or tradition, or rulers, or human nature – has become absorbed into the empire of individual self-determination, and so regarded as valid only if self-identified and self-endorsed. Not only have our moral ends become self-determined; so, too, has religion. Beauty has become a matter of individual taste rather than objective standards. Truth has widely come to be decreed as relative to how the individual sees things – 'my truth, your truth'; truth as 'a mobile army of metaphors', in Nietzsche's memorable phrase – rather than determined by impartial conditions on which universal agreement must, in principle, be expected, even if not in practice attained. Vocation is no longer handed down from one's forebears. More recently, sexual orientation and gender have increasingly been gathered into the realm of self-determination or self-identification – crucial dimensions of an identity that is, potentially, always a revisable work in progress.

Nonetheless, at each stage in the expansion of the autonomous subject, some areas of life have remained strictly out of bounds (whether for ever or for now we cannot know in advance). As of the time of writing, two areas that are still stipulated to be objectively given, and therefore on which individual autonomy – and the demand that its choices be respected and recognized – may not encroach, are age and ethnic identity. Those who have attempted to breach this taboo have discovered that self-identification is here as debarred as it is widely accepted as a sacred right in values, beauty, vocation, gender, sexual orientation, and truth. Émile Ratelband, a sixty-nine-year-old Dutch pensioner, TV personality, former politician, and self-described 'positivity guru', lost his battle in the courts to be legally recognized as forty-nine, the age he then felt he was – and was widely ridiculed for absurd, self-demeaning presumptuousness. Meanwhile, Rachel Dolezal, an American white academic who for decades passed herself off as being of Black and

Native American descent, and even managed to become a chapter president of the National Association for the Advancement of Colored People, one of the US's most prestigious Black civil rights organizations, was fired from her job and became a social pariah when it was discovered that she had no such heritage. Her claim to self-identify as 'trans-Black' in her 'internal sense of self', her 'essential essence', and her deepest values, was rejected as illegitimate.[4] In the unfolding story of Kantian autonomy, Ratelband and Dolezal were both deemed to have gone a big step too far.

This brief foray into the history of autonomy prompts the same question we asked about the cult of work: how could it possibly be an *engine* of procrastination? Doesn't its ever-expanding promise of agency and self-determination rather make it the opposite, in other words, a perfect antidote to procrastination?

The answer is that extravagant promises of autonomy which can't be realized intensify the sense that we're overwhelmed and ineffective, and so risk intensifying procrastination. Taken to their current extreme, such promises generate expectations of flawless control over our life and its purposes – expectations that we are, by nature and by rights, radically free to choose our priorities and then to implement them – which, if disappointed, foster a sense of impotence and undermine motivation.

And disappointed they're often bound to be. For, in reality, autonomy doesn't work with such mechanical reliability, either in setting our life priorities or in carrying them out. Life priorities are seldom chosen in a radically free way. From our earliest years they are deeply influenced by parents, peers, rivals, and the media. Moreover, they often reveal themselves only gradually and unconsciously, when we're ready for them and at a time that can't easily be predicted. Or they steal up on us, grabbing us with their charm. Or they transpire by chance opportunities to pursue them. Or we take notice of them only when we realize that they offer ready rewards, such as income and status.

Nor can we rely on looking inwards to discover our priorities and draw out our decisions. Our inner world is usually far from transparent; it yields only fitfully to direct introspection. 'Each [person] is furthest from himself', says Nietzsche – even remarking that we are 'necessarily strangers to ourselves, we do not comprehend ourselves, we *have* to misunderstand ourselves'.[5] To our 'chagrin', he adds, for we've been taught to expect that we have privileged access to our own souls. The famous maxim of the Delphic oracle, 'Know thyself!', is 'almost malicious', a cruel tease.[6]

We're therefore far from being as in command of setting our top priorities as today's extreme promises of autonomy tell us we are, or should be. In addition, multiple practical constraints can limit our choices, not least our choices of career or vocation; constraints such as insufficient educational credentials and connections, the need to earn money wherever we find the opportunity, the availability of housing, and responsibilities to others that drastically limit our options – to name a few. Once in work, our autonomy is assailed by the whims of bosses and the tyranny of targets. By the priority of fitting in over job satisfaction or the freedom to choose our projects. By the pressure in many professions to work ever longer hours to ever tighter deadlines – famously disproving John Maynard Keynes's prediction that people would be working a fifteen-hour week by 2030.[7] By rivals who – to paraphrase Gore Vidal –

don't just want to succeed but need us to fail. By lack of recognition, and by marginalization or exclusion from decision-making.

Nor can we easily change our field of work or reverse a decision to accept a job we dread, except at risk to our incomes, careers, and status. Other fields might no longer be open to us after certain ages; and even if they are, years of retraining are often needed, which can be unfeasible if we have a family to support and a mortgage to pay. For all who live under such constraints, the promise of self-determination can prove devastatingly empty.

A particularly intense expression of the cult of autonomy – and of how it can interact destructively with the cult of work – is to be found in the excesses of meritocracy, a term the sociologist Michael Young is credited with coining.[8] In contemporary times, dominated by the cults of autonomy and work, success is overwhelmingly ascribed to the self-governing individual who expresses their agency in the roll-call of achievements – especially wealth, status, and power – that they've won for themselves through merit. By dint of self-determination and self-responsibility, the 'winners' are seen – and widely see themselves – as morally deserving of their success while the 'losers' are seen – and often see themselves – as morally deserving of their failure.

This is the life brilliantly described by Michael Sandel in his book *The Tyranny of Merit*. It's a lie, Sandel argues, that upward mobility is available to anyone of sufficient talent, ingenuity, and effort, regardless of their background – and that it's therefore necessarily 'deserved'. In reality, meritocracy hasn't delivered the level playing field that, upholders claim, justifies its moral superiority over all other economic systems. Much of the success of the winners is down to the inherited privilege of ethnicity, class, and the luck of an upbringing that gets them into the best colleges and jobs, not least by bestowing on them, from an early age, the affluence for travel, extra tuition, sports training, theatre, and innumerable other horizon-widening activities that can be critical to gaining the credentials and confidence to access an elite education. In the process, the offspring of the affluent and well connected form their own networks of connections to supplement those they inherit from their parents.

As the beneficiaries of such financial, educational, and cultural privilege intermarry, and their own children in turn mix only with their own kind, so, Sandel fears, they develop into a kind of hereditary elite – a 'nepo' class, as it's sometimes called – of networked advantage that looks preponderantly after itself. As a psychologically and socially gated caste, they entrench ever greater inequality of opportunity and ever more separation from the rest of society whose social mobility they stymie and to whom they feel no connection or indebtedness. Refusing to acknowledge their privileges, they accept little obligation to aid the less fortunate, who inevitably lose out in the competition for resources.

As a result, meritocracy has promoted extreme inequality of opportunity and outcome, which makes millions of people feel unjustly excluded and so threatens the cohesion of whole societies. In evidence, Sandel cites the remarkable facts that in the US 'more than two-thirds of students at Ivy League schools come from the top 20 percent of the income scale' and at Princeton and Yale universities 'more students come from the top 1 percent than from the entire bottom 60 percent'.[9] This raging inequality helped ensure that most income growth over the four decades from the late 1970s to 2020 went to the top 10 per cent, with, notoriously, the richest 1 per cent of Americans making more than the entire bottom half.[10] The 'losers' in this system are trapped in their low incomes, struggling ever harder to maintain a basic standard of living and unable to ensure that their children fare better than they did. Seeing privileged kids effortlessly leapfrogging their own foments resentful cynicism, which in turn undermines motivation to pursue their own dreams and priorities – a perfect ecosystem for procrastination.

But the winners, we should add, are often trapped too. They're trapped in the demands of relentless striving and achievement and production for production's sake – sometimes in a field in which they've long lost interest. Imprisoned in an 'iron cage'[11] of time optimization, output maximization, and high consumption – albeit a gilded cage – they are held in their gleaming reality just as securely as the 'losers' are confined to their menial low-income jobs. The result of this system, whether you win or lose in it, is to stifle the freedom promised by autonomy, amid widespread burnout, depression, and ennui.

So is less work and more community the answer to the excesses of the cults of work and autonomy?

There are certainly stirrings of resistance to the cult of work in the growing clamour for a radical recalibration of the work–leisure balance, and increasing pockets of opposition to the cult of autonomy on the part of advocates for a more communitarian, less self-seeking, less meritocratic society. The conviction that to waste time is a crime against life – that one should boast of the hours one works and even of how little one sleeps – although still rampant, for example among some financial services elites, is slowly surrendering to an insistence that there's more to life than career and more to flourishing than individual success. Burgeoning disciplines like 'happiness economics' have developed indices of flourishing that assay human contentment in less narrow ways than income and output. At a practical level, resistance to the cult of work was strikingly expressed in the Great Resignation that followed the pandemic of 2020 and saw millions of people in Europe and America quit their jobs without quickly looking for new ones, inspired by the freedom and privacy discovered within an enforced home life where, for all its unwelcome isolation from colleagues and friends, a richer daily routine could be explored than one principally devoted to an employer organization.

Equally striking (and perhaps more durable) is the widespread demand to reduce the working week to four days. One prominent example arises from a study by a team of social scientists at Cambridge University in England and Boston College in the United States, together with other universities and the independent consultancy Autonomy, which reported in 2023.[12] Using data from, until then, 'the world's largest four-day working week trial', in which sixty-one organizations in the UK committed to a 20 per cent reduction in working hours for all staff for six months with no fall in wages, the authors conclude that the workers became fitter and more productive while maintaining and even slightly increasing their companies' revenues. The extra day off, in the words of the CEO of Autonomy, 'allowed you to be relaxed and rested, and ready to absolutely go for it on those other four days'.[13] It ensured that 'workers were much less inclined to kill time, and actively sought out technologies that improved their productivity', according to Professor Brendan Burchell, who led the University of Cambridge research. Burchell adds: 'Before the trial, many questioned whether we would see an increase in productivity to offset the reduction in working time – but this is exactly what we found.'[14]

But less work didn't just boost productivity and company revenues; it also had the tremendous benefit of enhancing the welfare of employees. Seventy-one per cent reported less burnout and 39 per cent said they were less stressed than at the beginning of the trial. Sick days fell by 65 per cent and the number of staff leaving the participating companies dropped by 57 per cent compared to the same period the previous year. Not surprisingly, work–life balance significantly improved, with 60 per cent of employees reporting that they could better combine their paid work with care responsibilities and an even greater percentage saying that they were better able to juggle work and social life.

It seems like working less is one answer to procrastination. After all, productivity was boosted, so employees were using the time available for work to get more done. Which makes sense; restricting the time permitted for a task can aid focus and discourage delay. We can't, of course, know if the boost would have endured for, say, a couple of years beyond the six months to which the Cambridge University/Boston College study was limited – in other words, once the freshness of a new schedule had worn off and its morale-uplifting sense of liberation from the arduous old one had faded. But even if it had endured – even if a shorter working week could sustainably boost productivity – it would still serve the cult of work, with its managerial-technocratic spirit. Indeed, it would do so all the more efficiently as that spirit would likely colonize the rebalanced life, entrenching itself in the extra time carved out for leisure, family, friends, and community, and ensuring that they were all experienced as work and as scheduled, managed downtime.

As a result, the new order would, in all probability, turn out to be no less rife with tedium and burnout. If, as the Cambridge study explicitly states, the very purpose of extra leisure and free time is to refresh employees for work, so that they can be 'absolutely ready to go for it on those other four days', it's likely that after an initial increase of contentment and productivity from the new-found extra freedom people would procrastinate just as much in four days as they did in five. Most traditional remedies to procrastination are proposed in this same spirit, which is why they seem attractive to our culture; but that's also why I doubt they offer a solution. Such recommendations aren't the alchemy that can convert intention into action.

The same is true of Michael Sandel's answer to the demoralization of winners and losers alike in the meritocratic system, namely greater equality secured through a dismantling of the extreme meritocratic society, more distributive government spending, and a return to a communitarian ethic of the common good. Urgent though it is that opportunities and benefits, in both income and status, be opened up more widely and fairly to the left behind, hemmed in by walls of hopelessness – splendid though it would be if these noble aims were achieved – such measures, in themselves, would leave the cults of work and autonomy exactly as they are now. They would still be the dominant markers of the successful self – still fundamental to our individual purpose, identity, and social standing – albeit with fairer distribution of the fruits of labour and perhaps less manic competitive striving. The ethic of self-rule through work and the imperative to be productive would be understood more in terms of contributing to the collective, as indeed is already the case in more socialized economies, such as those of Scandinavia and Switzerland. But their managerial-technocratic spirit would penetrate as deeply into life as a whole as they do in the most individualistic society.

Only *exiting that spirit* – at the heart of which lie the cults of autonomy and work as they've developed and are now practised in the West – will tackle procrastination at its roots. To do so we need to transform how we relate to those highest ends on which we're procrastinating; how we understand them, what we expect from them, how we focus on them – and, not least, what our avoidance of them is telling us. This is the moment to turn to my proposals for doing so.

PART II
Seven Ways to Unleash Motivation

4
Lower the Stakes

The problem with top priorities, vital though they are, is that their very significance can paralyse. So much rides on them – our sense of living a worthwhile life, our self-esteem and the esteem of others, even our physical and mental health – that we can quickly become overwhelmed by their stakes. Our mind, agitated and unable to focus, yearns to wander free of the chains that tie it to its own treasured goals. We're supposed to feel in command of our power to choose – and to execute – what we prioritize, but we feel trapped by the importance we've invested in it. The constant pressure of deadlines and targets exacerbates that trapped feeling and worsens anxiety – the deadliest cause of procrastination. As Bertrand Russell (1872–1970) quipped, 'One of the symptoms of an approaching nervous breakdown is the belief that one's work is so terribly important, and that [even] to take a holiday would bring all kinds of disaster.'[1]

In this situation, we need to junk the conventional advice that tells us to keep the urgency of our priorities at the front of our minds if we're to stop procrastinating. Instead, we should do the opposite: free our minds of their tyranny. Keep our focus on them while imaginatively defusing their overpowering significance. If they are priorities to which we're genuinely committed, we will retain our innate motivation to pursue them, but without being daunted by their importance.

There are as many ways of doing this as our imagination is able to supply, and each reader will have their own; but here are mine.

The first step on the way to lightening the significance of our top priorities – to making them less intimidating – is to recast them as our favoured displacement activities. Now the motivation we discover in them is that they enable us to avoid weightier tasks. We re-envision them as an escape from – a way of procrastinating over – what we 'should' be doing. Instead of experiencing them as heavy responsibilities (to ourselves, to peers, to parents and family), they're there to sneak off and have fun with while we sideline everything else. The early twentieth-century humourist Robert Benchley put it perfectly: 'Anyone can do any amount of work provided it isn't the work he is supposed to be doing at the moment'.[2]

In other words, when a project's significance is weighing us down, we should try to flip our perspective on it through 180 degrees. We should reimagine it as our way of avoiding a much bigger priority; the crucial one that really needs to get done. We then experience it as our infidelity to that other one which ought to be commanding our sole focus and which is like the only prisoner in a panopticon, the legendary jail where an inmate is under relentless scrutiny by the authorities, watched at all times of the day and night. With this project, by contrast, we're liberated from that kind of spotlight. We can plunge into it or set it aside as the whim takes us, exploring our interests freely and following them wherever they lead.

It's a trick that can work well for a while. But there's still more we can do to lower the stakes of a priority. We can focus only on the moment-by-moment pleasure of pursuing it – only on the sheer enjoyment, *right now*, that it permits our powers of expression and experiment. We don't defer the satisfactions of working on it to a time when it has been successfully completed, so that we're always living for rewards that are yet to come. Nor do we work on it in order to fulfil others' expectations of us – or even our own expectations of ourselves: for expectations, too, are intrinsically future-directed. Nor, by the same token, are we focused on meeting deadlines and goals, which always lie ahead of us until they're attained. Our aim, on the contrary, is to detach our mind, at least temporarily, from the despotism of the future and of ticking time.

There's surely no better way than the intimacy of a purely present focus to put us in touch with our innate motivation. It doesn't entail forgetting where we're heading. On the contrary, it's the most vivid and immediate way of rediscovering the living force of our hopes and commitments. We remain clear about our goal; indeed, it imbues the present with orientation and meaning and excitement. But now the goal is there as a gentle guide – not thundering down on us with its urgency. I will return to this point in Chapter 9.

Here's an example of how our powers can be liberated by experiencing a top priority as a substitute activity – not tyrannized by deadlines and other time-management pressures. In a normal working week, I try to carve out uninterrupted time for writing by reserving four hours a day for it and it alone – with no other duties and without yielding to the temptation to get lesser tasks out of the way so as to clear the decks for what most matters to me.

Sometimes this aids my writing; at other times I end up procrastinating nonetheless. One week, during the writing of this book, I was scheduled to fly to a conference in the US, the first stop on a three-week trip, for which I still needed to finish preparing a demanding talk. But a few days before leaving I developed mild but painful sciatica and was told by my doctor to postpone my departure for a week to avoid exacerbating it by a long flight followed by more sitting at a two-day conference. Unexpectedly, I was plunged into an organizational vacuum – a dimensionless stretch of time with no schedule, no obligations, no limits to the time available for writing. Only a now. Normally, this would precipitate a procrastination nightmare; instead, the opposite happened. I'd seldom worked so easily and fluently.

The reason was no mystery. Because I was working on my book instead of what I was supposed to be doing and because I was free from my habitual self-imposed obligation to spend four hours a day on it, come what may, somehow the pressure I felt to make progress with the manuscript temporarily lifted. Anxiety about not leading my life well if my attention to it flagged was relieved. Delight in the privilege of thinking and self-expression for its own sake took the place of the finger-wagging threat to my sense of fulfilment if I procrastinated.

In this case, the freedom created by enforced circumstances had unlocked innate motivation. What if I could achieve this at will?

For a few weeks, this is exactly what I attempted. I imagined that writing the book was just freewheeling fun, a pleasurable distraction from what I ought to be doing, and unencumbered by deadlines – the very opposite of most advice for overcoming procrastination. This released me from constantly thinking about the future achievement of my task and allowed me the peace of mind that I needed to make headway.

The paradox of committing to a top priority enforced by deadlines is that it can demotivate by relentlessly bringing into view the mountain of what's still to be achieved. Deadlines can also fill our mind with the tyrannical passing of time, day by day, hour by hour – time which always feels like it's running away too fast to complete the project on schedule. Trying to ignore those deadlines won't, of course, work all the time, or for everyone, but it's one way of reducing what can be the destructive urgency of top priorities and their servitude to the ambition of a life optimally lived. It accounts for the fact that this book exists at all.

What, though, if such imaginative downgrading of our priorities – with its related attempts to free ourselves of the anxiety of deadlines and of living primarily for the sake of future accomplishments – doesn't do the trick? What then?

Then we need to pursue another way of lowering oppressively high stakes: we need to become less focused on whether or not they will secure the esteem of others – and less prone to shame if they don't. While craving esteem can be highly motivating, taken to excess it's among the most potent causes of procrastination. As the psychologists Rhonda Fee and June Tangney argue, 'Shame-prone individuals, who are especially fearful of negative evaluations . . . may be especially motivated to put off the "moment of abysmal truth" – delaying, avoiding, and procrastinating.'[3]

To crave esteem (and to fearfully anticipate the shame of failing) is always to worry about what happens *after* our project is completed. It's to fret about the recognition it will garner, the status it will secure for us, the contempt falling short might evoke. All that anxiety for what is to come pulls our attention away from present absorption in the project and turns it into a means of securing applause. As a result, it's no longer fully ours and we lose that special intimacy – that delicious cocoon of privacy and dialogue – with what we really care about, which allows it to lead us to unexpected destinations. This is another way, so common to modern life, in which we sacrifice real presence in the now for rewards deferred to the future.

Which leads to the other problem with pursuing our priorities to gain the approval of others: how they will regard us, and even whether they will notice us at all, is hard and often impossible to influence. Famously, Elvis Presley was repeatedly rejected by record companies at the outset of his career. Similarly, J. K. Rowling's first Harry Potter book was turned down by twelve publishers before being accepted by the independent publisher Bloomsbury. Anne Frank's diary was refused by ten publishers. Stephen King, The Beatles, Alexander Graham Bell's invention of the telephone – they all met with initial scepticism and even rejection.

A modicum of recognition is a basic human need. Being seen and endorsed and respected, not just for our qualities but, even more fundamentally, for our very existence – that we are there at all as members of our communities – is vital, from earliest infancy onwards, to the constitution of our selfhood. But although potentially highly energizing, the need for recognition can and often does end up as a destructive and insatiable addiction, in which every shot of recognition leaves even the most successful craving more. Then far from being a source of freedom – among the deepest of all sources of freedom – social recognition becomes a form of imprisonment by the expectations, whims, and fancies of others. Our most personal commitments become hostages to their approval – as we mould and even abandon our own values to suit theirs and as their esteem for us becomes the foundation of our esteem for ourselves. The perverse result is to *drain* us of selfhood, identity, and freedom – the very blessings that we seek from others' recognition.

Kicking the addiction can be made a lot easier by realizing that even the most extravagant esteem of our peers can be very superficial. And very transitory. The reality is that most people aren't *that* interested in what we do or achieve. They've got their own strivings, successes, and failures to worry about. Many will be tied down by commitments to families and jobs, pleasures and troubles, which leave them little time to really see and engage with us. And to the extent they do engage, their attention won't be for long. The successes of others will soon displace ours. As Marcus Aurelius, Roman emperor from 161 to 180 CE, put it in an aphorism titled 'On Fame': 'See how, just as drifting sands constantly overlay the previous sand, so in our lives what we once did is very quickly covered over by subsequent layers.'[4]

The often-paralysing pointlessness of chasing after esteem is perennially true – as valid in our day as it was in Marcus Aurelius's. It's probably *more valid* in these times of ever-greater individualism – despite the explosion of social media and its opportunities for getting noticed. For the invention of autonomy in the eighteenth century hasn't only conferred the blessing that our values and identities can increasingly be defined by us alone (and repeatedly redefined over the course of our lives), rather than allocated by society or determined by birth. It has also brought extraordinary vulnerability because the more autonomous we are – the more our values might diverge from everyone else's – the more others' esteem for us needs to be tailored to who *each of us, as an individual, takes ourself to be*; to what we value, and to what we've achieved. The contentedness afforded by the esteem of others, always fleeting and fragile, becomes still more elusive when those who bestow it are expected to see, understand, and value us with such bespoke, personalized precision.

Of course, even in our increasingly individualistic world some recognition is still accorded us purely as members of a group. Clearly, inherited status determined by the class, race, and family we were born into by no means disappeared with the end of feudalism. But today we take ourselves to be, first and foremost, self-determining, and so we want the esteem we're accorded to be geared to who we are and have chosen to be. Even celebrity 'nepo' offspring, hugely privileged in the recognition stakes by their inherited prestige, and often basking in it, don't want to be famous and recognized just because of who their parents are. They want to be seen and lauded, above all, for who they are.

But here's the rub. Autonomy cuts two ways. Sure, we all – you and I and everyone else – want and expect recognition tailored to our unique individuality, and in this rat race we're in competition with countless other individuals who are also curating their profile in order to be noticed and affirmed in their uniqueness. At the same time, of course, the people whose recognition we seek are themselves autonomous and have as much right as we do to determine what and who they value. Which means that they're free *not* to esteem us, or even to notice us. If their sights are elsewhere or if our priorities and achievements are not to their taste, how can we possibly expect them to sincerely esteem who we've chosen to be? (And sincere all esteem must be; for sincerity is a vital ingredient in esteem, its absolute precondition, without which it's worthless – or, worse, manipulative and mocking.)

In short, the cult of autonomy and our need for recognition are often in fundamental conflict. The cult of autonomy makes us deeply needy of others' bespoke recognition, but it also makes that bespoke recognition vulnerable to their own sovereign values and choice. And so it threatens to strand us, unseen and unheard, in a lonely desert of our own uniqueness. Which in turn creates the intense temptation to abandon the project of self-creation; to give up on achieving our own priorities, to cave in to the preferences of our peers, and to pimp our choice of goals to whoever seems likely to bestow their esteem most readily on us. It's a temptation that was clearly understood by such founders of the ideal of personal autonomy as Jean-Jacques Rousseau (1712–78), who lamented that the modern individual lives 'always outside himself, knows how to live only in the opinion of others' and finds that it is 'from their judgement alone that he draws the sentiment of his own existence'.[5] If this was true in eighteenth-century Geneva, how much truer it is in an age of social media, in which we are ever more forcefully persuaded that to be someone is to exist in the eyes of others, not just those we know and trust but potentially unlimited numbers of strangers.

The only way out of this bind is to keep our hunger for recognition within firm limits – shaking off excessive dependency on it, so that, as far as possible, we're happy if it comes but indifferent if it doesn't. For many of us, the resulting sense of freedom to pursue our own projects in our own way – and to find that renewed sense of intimacy with them to which I alluded before – is one of the keys to overcoming procrastination. It's a freedom to return to ourselves, so that we can find joy in our commitments for their own sake. It's a freedom to be content with (if we're lucky) one loved one who really sees us in our individuality, and who says to us 'Here I am!'

In Leonard Cohen's words from 'Dance Me to the End of Love', 'Let me see your beauty when the witnesses are gone'.

In addition to being recognized by our peers and contemporaries, there's a further craving for significance that can seize us and force our projects into its service: the all too human ambition to be recognized by our descendants; to leave a trace of our individual life that will survive and grant us – our deeds and character – a kind of immortality. So that we will not simply be cancelled by death. It's a craving that can be highly motivating: but it, too, readily fosters procrastination as we come to realize how elusive it is; how it further raises the stakes of our priorities in a way that we can't control; how it distracts us from enjoying them for their own sake.

The kinds of immortality that people have sought have likely been almost as various as the cultures of the world. It might be feats of heroism, as it has been for warriors since ancient times. Or it might be creative achievements, from scientific discoveries to triumphs of engineering, from literature to architecture. Or it might be the legacy of our loving and being loved: children in whose lives and memories we will endure; relationships with partners, friends, and spouses who will remember us; acts of altruism and service that make the world a better place for future generations. Or, especially in the social media era, it might be a lifestyle, a gesture, a scream, an outrageous remark that is sufficiently extreme, unexpected, and flamboyant to be noticed above millions of competing voices. The hope is not just to live our 'best possible self'– or at least our most visible possible self – for the sake of our own fulfilment in this life; it's also to secure a place in the memory of those who come after us that will be a tribute to our unique existence – and that will last beyond a handful of sympathetic descendants in the first generation after our death.

It's a hope for eventual recognition that, again, can powerfully motivate – but only if we don't focus too clearly on the minuscule probability that it will actually be fulfilled – or on the even more minuscule probability that, if it is fulfilled, our legacy won't be mangled in the memory of our successors. As W. H. Auden's great poem 'In Memory of W. B. Yeats' warns, from the moment of his death Yeats lost all control over how his life's work would be assimilated by others. Instead 'he became his admirers'; he became whatever each of them made of him, his immense achievements 'scattered among a hundred cities / And wholly given over to unfamiliar affections'. 'The words of a dead man', adds Auden ominously, 'Are modified in the guts of the living'.[6]

Unfortunately, the likelihood that our reality will either be forgotten or mangled by subsequent generations, as they appropriate our life piecemeal, usually dawns on us ever more clearly as we grow older and as the time to make an impact gets shorter. If our achievements should happen to live on, they too will be ingested, digested, and turned into whoever our admirers or detractors are. We might try to deny these mortal realities, but our defences against them are seldom watertight.

Modified in the guts of the living or not, any vivid memory of us is unlikely to last beyond, at the very most, the third or fourth generations after our death. They, in turn, will be replaced by countless future generations to whom our achievements will be completely unknown, uninteresting, and possibly – in view of their having quite different values to ours today – meaningless or repugnant. Even the most epoch-making creators often, perhaps usually, vanish into quick obscurity soon after their demise. Who, except specialists in the field, now knows the names of the inventors of antibiotics, space rockets, and jet aircraft, or of most artists, singers, composers, or CEOs who were legends in their own lifetimes? How many of the leading politicians of just a few decades ago, or of the great kings and queens of history, are remembered today by their compatriots? How many of the founders of the largest charities? How many of the writers who populated the bestseller lists? A book-devouring novelist I know, who claims to have reviewed every *New York Times* bestseller list since its founding almost a century ago, in 1931, was astonished to discover that he hadn't heard of over half its authors, let alone read them. A distinguished professor of pharmacology remarked to me that he couldn't name all the living winners of the Nobel Prize in medicine, never mind the dead ones. Marcus Aurelius again puts it succinctly when he exclaims: 'How many who once rose to fame are now consigned to oblivion; and how many who sang their fame are long disappeared!'[7]

If such Olympians vanish into obscurity, we can be sure that the overwhelming majority of us will soon disappear without trace, no matter how impressive our legacy and even if our name should one day be commemorated in some nook, on a roll-call of the distinguished, idly glimpsed by the occasional passer-by to whom it means nothing. So that to freight our priorities with the hope of lasting renown is to lumber them with what is almost certainly a pointless illusion.

To realize and accept this reality can be immediately empowering, just as it can be to shed an addiction to recognition in the eyes of our contemporaries. It allows us to take back the power of judgement over our lives that we surrendered to others by needing the thought of their esteem in order to esteem ourselves. We therefore reclaim, in a certain sense, our own existence, the recognition – and to that extent even the reality – of which we'd subcontracted to unknowable strangers. Coming home to ourselves in this way can fill us with renewed motivation to be the author of our lives.

That such self-sufficiency can be liberating is akin to the freedom that swathes of Western society have found in banishing from the cosmos an omnipotent, all-seeing God who was widely taken to guarantee (whether unconditionally or conditional upon obedience to his ordinances) loving witness and acceptance to each of us, down to the most secret depths of our being – and to do so not only in the present but for eternity. Instead of a life oriented towards this extravagant promise, modern individuals have increasingly claimed independence from such a divine source of recognition along with the intrusive inspection and judgement of their most private feelings and desires that necessarily accompanied it.

One cost of sacrificing the security of divine recognition is to see ourselves as transient specks in an impersonal universe. Although many, such as Blaise Pascal (1623–62), have been terrified by this cosmic picture, innumerable others, like Nietzsche and the twentieth-century writer Albert Camus, have thrilled to it. For them, the vision of humanity's aloneness in, as Pascal put it, 'the infinite immensity of spaces whereof I know nothing, and which knows nothing of me',[8] has evoked terror and awe that is, in its own way, as intense as that traditionally reserved for the divine. It's an awe that has only become more marked as science reveals the ever-deeper strangeness of nature, to which our everyday experience and concepts afford little or no access, and uncovers mysteries that might be in principle insoluble. And it's reflected in the palpable relish with which contemporary thinkers describe humanity's insignificance to nature as 'a mote of dust in the morning sky' (Carl Sagan), or as 'chemical scum on a moderate-sized planet, orbiting around a very average star in the outer suburb of one among a hundred billion galaxies' (Stephen Hawking).[9]

This vision of our puny but defiant insignificance, outstaring a meaningless cosmos that is totally indifferent to us, can be strangely energizing. It throws us back on our own devices – on our own talents and powers and all too human yearnings for a meaningful home in the world – not only as individuals but also, collectively, as communities and even as a species, marooned on one among billions of planets. And so it can inspire in us a sense of radical freedom, driving us to overcome all procrastination that stands in the way of our becoming who we really are in this one brief life.

So much for lowering the stakes of our top priorities by finding freedom from the expectations and esteem of others, namely our peers or descendants. Can we also unshackle motivation by lightening our own expectations of ourselves? In particular, can we lower the stakes by avoiding destructive perfectionism?

If by destructive perfectionism we mean that we set standards for the attainment of our most cherished priorities that are unreachably high – precisely because we value those priorities so greatly – there's no doubt that the answer is yes. Whether we set unreachable standards from the moment we embark on a priority or whether every time we're in sight of achieving it we raise our sights still higher, convinced that we can and should always do better, such perfectionism is a major cause of (and excuse for!) procrastination. Fearing failure, we procrastinate in order to avoid the disappointment and humiliation we've set up for ourselves.

For example, if I'm unable to move on to the next sentence of a book I'm writing until I judge the current one to be fully precise, polished, vivid, original, and a seamless part of a compelling whole, I will more than likely get stuck. The little I've written will become stiff, constipated, overworked, and so will demand further revision. Which will likely feel inadequate, and, in turn, set in train more unproductive tinkering. A vicious circle whirls into motion, in which tinkering and demoralization feed each other. Even if I can keep improving the fragment of my project that I'm stuck on now, a huge stretch of it still lies ahead and the challenge of ever getting to the end overwhelms me. Ultimately, this pressure can lead beyond the frustrations of paralysis to complete burnout.

Nor is the hunt for perfection limited to our work projects. It's rampant in the world of romantic relationships, where people might toy with each other for years, frozen in hesitation, as they imagine or discover limitations in each other; or fear that they will in the future; or worry that sharing their life – with all the unpredictable vulnerabilities and responsibilities that can bring, from financial troubles to illness and aging – will hamper another priority, such as career, or freedom to explore the world. Wrenched by their alternating yeses, noes and maybes, despite believing that they've found the love of their lives, they continue prevaricating, either at a distance from each other or while living outwardly together but inwardly apart.

Or they give up and move on. Which doesn't entail that the matter is closed. Like all procrastination over our deepest desires, we're not necessarily done with what we've avoided. For years afterwards, we might worry whether we did the right thing. Were we cowardly in the face of what we know: that the world isn't hospitable to perfection? That the ideal usually survives only in our imagination? That we cannot predict the future and have little power over it? That compromise with reality is a precondition for making anything real?

Although it's likely that perfectionism has always caused people to procrastinate, studies suggest that both it and procrastination have mushroomed in recent decades. 'Irrational ideals of the perfect self have become desirable – even necessary – in a world where performance, status and image define a person's usefulness and value', according to psychologists Thomas Curran and Andrew P. Hill. Surveying almost 42,000 American, Canadian, and British college students over the twenty-seven years between 1989 and 2016, they found a huge, 32 per cent, increase in 'socially prescribed' perfectionist attitudes, driven by cultural expectations and adopted by parents, peers, and elite educational institutions, along with a 10 per cent increase in 'self-oriented perfectionism'.[10] That such expectations are likely to boost procrastination is confirmed by other studies showing that the perfectionism they incite substantially reduces the effectiveness of intentions to implement one's priorities.[11]

It seems obvious that the solution to procrastination rooted in perfectionism is to dial down standards that we are almost inevitably going to fail to meet. To say to ourselves, 'Stop demanding unrealistic perfection! The best job you can do for now will have to do!'

This is certainly right. But the problem with perfectionism goes beyond the paralysing fear of failure caused by setting unattainable standards for ourselves. The very idea of perfection can be an illusion, namely, that it's possible to say what it would be to achieve a goal such that no further improvement is possible. For example, would a singer ever be able to specify in all details what *the* perfect singer is, so that they could, in principle, reach a point where they say 'Now I am a perfect singer. It's impossible – for me (or perhaps for anyone) – to do better than this!'? Or even, 'Now I sing this particular song perfectly!'? Similarly, I might think that I know what a perfect sentence or romantic partner or garden would look like. Or, at least, I might think that I'd recognize them if I encountered them. But do I? And would I?

For sure, I can find some fault here and there with anything and anyone. There will always be something that could be improved on. But that's not the same as saying that I have a vision of their perfection – just as people often flee relationships when they discover blemishes in their partner, but without knowing precisely what they want or what would finally satisfy them.

The intrinsic vagueness of much perfectionism is reflected

in how researchers define it. For example, 'Perfectionism is broadly defined as a combination of excessively high personal standards and overly critical self-evaluations', says one group of psychologists.[12] Or, says another: 'When directed toward the self, individuals attach irrational importance to being perfect, hold unrealistic expectations of themselves, and are punitive in their self-evaluations.'[13]

But words like 'excessive', 'overly', 'irrational', and 'unrealistic' are unhelpfully vague. Perfection seems a little like the concept of infinity: it is intuitively meaningful until we focus in on it.

For Aristotle, one of the earliest theoreticians of perfection, to be perfect is to be a complete instance of one's kind. It is, for example, to be a complete human being, a complete flute player, a complete doctor – such that no exemplar of the kind could be better. In his words, it is 'that which in respect of excellence and goodness cannot be excelled in its kind'.[14] But how are we to specify this condition? What would a 'completed' or 'perfect' me look like? A me so good that nothing – given the kind of person I am, or given the kind of being *Homo sapiens* is – could be better? No wonder we get stuck and procrastinate, if it's such a goal that we're aiming at.

In a similarly extravagant vein, various pioneers of the eighteenth-century European Enlightenment, such as the French thinker, the Marquis de Condorcet, spoke of the perfectibility of humankind, a project on which their intellectual descendants have perhaps never entirely given up, despite the constricting narrowness of any predetermined ideal of perfection – not to mention the overwhelming evidence of human beings' incorrigible dispositions to cruelty, bigotry, pride, and betrayal, underpinned by prodigious powers of denial and self-justification, among numerous other reasons for their imperfectibility. Similarly, hundreds of books in the last three centuries have offered recipes for becoming the ideal parent – which, as we see every day, burdens parents with the unfulfillable and often crushing expectation that raising children is a perfectible skill, especially in regard to a child's moral and emotional education.

Why, then, do we persist in holding to the destructive illusion that the goal of perfection can so often be, given its costs in debilitating procrastination? One reason is the value we attach to our top priorities, so that the more valuable a priority is to us the higher the standards we set for achieving it. Another is pressure from the wider culture; pressure that, as Curran and Hill's survey suggests, is particularly prevalent today, issuing from parents, educational institutions, and a fiercely competitive meritocratic system that attributes wealth, status, and other forms of success exclusively to individual effort and talent. A third is a craving for control over the vulnerability intrinsic to life – not least, as we discussed earlier in this chapter, our vulnerability to how others see us; to their rejecting or ignoring us. According to the psychiatrist Allan Mallinger, at the heart of perfectionism is a myth that goes like this:

> I can (and must) always perform with flawless competence, make the right choice or decision, excel in everything that counts and never be found wrong about anything. I can be, and should be, above criticism in every important personal attribute, including my values, attitudes and opinions. Thus, I can guarantee myself fail-safe protection against failure, criticism, rejection and humiliation, any of which would be unbearable.[15]

Related to this search for control is a further motive for seeing ourselves as devotees of perfection, namely pride. I flatter myself that my standards are so high that rather than settling for anything less than fully attaining them, I will stall on this project, right here, until I get just right what I've done so far. Or I'll take a temporary break from the whole project to recharge myself for a fresh return to it. Or I'll simply give up. It's easier on my self-respect to do nothing rigorously than something inadequately. Unlike those who compromise their standards, I'm delaying out of an abundance of diligence and integrity. I can therefore respect myself as someone who has the courage to be contemptuous of themselves – contemptuous of their failure to achieve their exalted ideals. Or, as Nietzsche brilliantly puts it: 'Whoever despises himself still respects himself as one who despises.'[16]

Yet the procrastination that is engendered by the search for perfection – the conceit that masquerades as modesty – can lead to paralysis and thence to depression so incapacitating that, instead of the best, we get not merely the adequate but nothing at all. In failing to secure control over life's contingency, and therefore to avoid the anxiety of vulnerability, it can foment far worse anxiety still as well as severe damage to one's self-esteem and esteem in the eyes of others. As a result, perfectionists often abandon in advance ends they most want to pursue – ends on which they're sure they will fail; and they avoid any interaction with those who might be witnesses to this failure. As Mallinger puts it, they therefore 'sacrifice fulfilment, productivity, creativity, intimacy, and spontaneity in their pursuit of a non-existent guarantee of security'.[17]

Alternatively, the perfectionist persists with their illusory search, and in doing so risks ending up with lifeless, if pristine-looking, results. A cautionary tale is the design and construction of a house in Vienna that Ludwig Wittgenstein worked on for his sister between 1927 and 1929. Excellence was not good enough for the fastidious philosopher. As he himself said: 'I am not interested in erecting a building, but in . . . presenting to myself the *foundations of all possible buildings*.'[18] The sociologist Richard Sennett observes of this ambition: 'No more grandiose project can be imagined. The young philosopher set himself out to understand the nature of all architecture and to build something exemplary, perfect . . .'[19]

It turned out to be the only building that Wittgenstein ever designed (apart from a house he used for writing in rural Norway). His devotion to this vision of its perfection knew few bounds. In a story related by his niece Hermine Wittgenstein, 'he had the ceiling of a large room raised by three centimeters [a little over one inch], just when it was almost time to start cleaning the completed house' – a tinkering with proportions that involved huge and expensive structural changes.[20]

The result, as Wittgenstein himself reflected many years later, was that the building lacked 'primordial life'. In a note to himself of 1940, he excoriated his own creation, writing that it 'lacks health' and merely has 'good manners'[21] – implying that far from being in some sense perfect, it was merely correct. Or, as Sennett puts it, his 'relentlessness deformed it'.[22]

The moral? Abandon the illusion that the perfect end product may be defined in advance in all its details. This is as true of an individual project as it is of our life itself. The perfect novel, the perfect sound for a violin, the perfect aircraft, the perfect table – no such thing can be specified or attained, such that – as Aristotle puts it – nothing of its kind could be better or more complete. Instead of an inflexible blueprint, have in mind at every stage a revisable working plan for the whole – a vision of the contours and the spirit of the end product that provides a road map from which deviation is possible; a road map towards a destination that is discovered only in the striving.

In summary, the danger of perfectionism that imagines it has an exhaustively defined and predetermined goal which cannot be improved upon isn't just that it can paralyse us when we inevitably fall short of it. Nor merely that it ignores our individual limitations. It's also that in any priority, project, or relationship, this kind of perfectionism is a prison of fixed ideas – and often a prison of mirages – in the service of which we stifle experiment, evolution, individuality, spontaneity, the irregular, the playful, and the unexpected. It locks us into a single, rigid way forward that we deludedly take to be the path to 'the ultimate'. And it distracts us from the real perfection, which lies in the journey. It lies in the passion to search and to discover – to experiment with and to revise, perhaps over a lifetime of struggle – what it means for us, as the individual we are, to genuinely live a form of life, like being an architect or a musician, in the time and place we inhabit and with the talents, dispositions, energies, and health at our disposal.

But on any given project I still need to have the intuition that this is as good as I can do for the time being – that this is good enough – and stop there.

5
Remember We Are Mortal

In the previous chapter we proposed that one way to imaginatively lower the stakes of our most deeply held priorities, and so avoid procrastinating over them, is not to burden them with the expectation of securing a legacy that will survive our death. The reality, we said, is that death soon terminates almost all reputations, if not all memory that we ever existed.

But this is only half the story of how recognizing the reality of death as a terminus can enable us to experience our individual existence more vigorously and to live our life more authentically. The other half works very differently. Rather than lowering the stakes of our priorities by minimizing our concern with the judgement of posterity, it raises their stakes by bringing to immediate and maximal awareness the reality of our own death as the horizon – and ever-present possibility – that marks the end of all our options to act and to be. For if we can genuinely internalize this awareness – a supremely difficult task! – and allow it to penetrate deeply enough into us, it can transform and reinvigorate our relation to ourselves, to the priorities that structure our life, and to the world.

What does this mean?

It means, most basically, that experiencing myself as

mortal is at the heart of why people and projects and life itself have meaning for me. And of how they matter to me. It is the inevitability of death that gives my commitments to them maximal force. What I want to claim in this chapter is that to experience myself as mortal requires much more than merely accepting death as a hopefully far-off event that seems thoroughly unreal right now. For such acceptance is too tepid to be more than briefly or sporadically effective in motivating us. Rather we need to go far beyond it towards attaining a deep awareness of death's possibility *at any moment* – the kind of awareness of death that alone can powerfully inspire motivation and so overcome procrastination.

I will need to disentangle and explain these claims in a few steps.

First, the ways in which we usually think we're facing the inevitability of death fall into the tepid category. Most take the form of affirmation – matter of fact, defiant, or fearful – that 'we're all going to die eventually', perhaps allied to a refusal of any consolation of post-mortem existence or an afterlife free of suffering. But such affirmation still banishes death to a realm of quasi-abstraction, where it becomes somehow real only when it happens to *other* people – unless those other people are those we love so deeply that when they die a part of us dies with them. (How else to account for the subliminal euphoria that is sometimes palpable at funeral receptions, which, if we're honest about it, is motivated by the mourners' relief that it's someone else, and not them, who's in the coffin?)

Another tepid form of accepting the reality of death is to alight on a vivid way to appreciate the brevity of life. One of the best is Oliver Burkeman's recasting of a span of, say, eighty years as four thousand weeks. To realize that, if we're forty, we have only two thousand weeks left – assuming that, in global terms, we're one of the luckier ones – can shock us into realizing that we'll never do everything we'd like to do, and should get on with formulating and pursuing our top priorities. But can it provide the motivation to really *live* them fully? And, crucially too, does the shock effect endure? I certainly find that it's effective at first, for a few days or, at best, a month at a time; but that it quickly wears off after that, no matter how often I remind myself of my appallingly few remaining weeks. Here, too, our internalization of the reality of death remains too feeble for it to provide sustained motivation to live our life fully.

The same is true for the painful reality that we necessarily die alone; that nobody can die in our stead when our end comes; that others might comfort us in our dying, mourn our passing, and even feel that part of them has died with us; but it is only we who will be the subject of our death.

These tepid ways of acknowledging death don't go nearly far enough to bring us into a relation to our mortality that can unleash motivation. On the contrary, they all push awareness of death out into a blurry future, which has little grip over us in the present, however much we theoretically 'know' that our time is limited.

For death to motivate, it needs to play a much more intimate and immediate role in our lives. Not as the end point of our existence that seems so unreal to us now, but as an ever-present possibility that stands before us right here. This, as I understand it,[1] is the profound insight of the twentieth-century philosopher Martin Heidegger, who tells us that only a life structured by such intimate awareness of what, in his opaque language, he calls 'the possibility of the absolute impossibility'[2] of existence can be authentic, and so jolt us into our true individuality. Only in my resolute preparedness for a death that can arrive in an hour, a day, ten years, fifty years, or whatever – a death that will be ineluctably mine to the extent that nothing else can be – *only then am I able to become a self and to truly live as an individual*. In the absence of such preparedness, we might add, the cult of autonomy cannot begin to open the way to individual authenticity. Rather, it merely seduces and deludes us to believing that we are living authentically, while, in reality, we are lost in the concerns and chatter of the anonymous crowd, passively tailoring our priorities to theirs.

But, wait a minute, we might say, surely dwelling on the possibility that our death can come at any moment would immobilize us in panic? Far from revealing our true priorities in life, unleashing motivation to pursue them, and inspiring authentic individuality, wouldn't it merely demoralize us, rendering all striving and choice meaningless, and fostering resignation and/or a dash for random aims and pleasures? All of which would worsen procrastination.

The answer is yes only if that awareness of death takes the form of a panicked *carpe diem*. Panic might trigger bursts of activity, but it seldom sustains the attention needed to carry through long-term priorities. On the contrary, it confuses, exhausts, and paralyses.

As I've been suggesting, however, there's another way of relating to the reality that death can come to me at any moment. It's to seek an intense intimacy with that reality until we reach a point where the possibility that tomorrow nothing more will be possible inspires calm attentiveness rather than panicked haste. This is a point where such intimacy with our mortality endows our life and our priorities and our every moment with a meaning – a validity – guaranteed by the simple fact of our existence right now. This is an unassailable meaning that stands in no need of justification. It suffuses our awareness with the thrilling power of our being-here, so that nothing we do or experience, however routine, can be trivial or insignificant.

This state of awareness is hard to put into words, but if we let it come to us it can powerfully inspire motivation in a way that tepid ways of accepting death's ultimate inevitability cannot achieve. Indeed, far from motivating us, tepid acceptance can undermine motivation and frighten us into procrastinating. Let me give a personal example of how this can happen.

I began to be puzzled in my teens that just the *prospect* of making a major life choice – in particular of a vocation or a spouse – could conjure in my imagination the frightening spectre of death. As a result, I was tempted back then to avoid long-term commitments of any kind. But, I wondered, why was I reacting in this strange way? Surely great decisions are a sign of freedom – of life – not a portend of death? Perhaps, I thought, the answer was that to choose is necessarily to close down other options; that the frightening thing was recognizing that I could never do everything I craved, however long I might realistically live. Then I realized that the reason was different: a choice that will set the course of my life – and therefore that is, at least as I intend it at the outset, to last until I die – brutally reminds me that I'm on a trajectory that will end in unceremonious extinction. It makes the trajectory vivid in a way that shunning a commitment doesn't. It forces me to face the irreversibility of time. It's another ratchet on the path that will one day culminate in my ceasing to be. Yet rather than dwelling on this experience of mortality and allowing myself to become progressively more familiar with it, I'd recoil from doing so, succumbing instead to the magical thinking that to avoid choice is to avoid the spectre of death.

What I later came to understand, thanks to Martin Heidegger, is that many if not most ways of grasping death either keep it safely vague or demoralize us by draining our priorities of meaning – by posing the question 'why does anything I accomplish matter if I'm going to die?' And that affirmation of death's ultimate inevitability is more frightening than deep immersion in its ever-present possibility. For, in practice, only such deep immersion can be the alchemy that turns paralysis by fear of death into inspiration by anticipation of death. Only such deep immersion can turn an essentially unfree self into a genuinely free self – a self that, according to Heidegger, is free to choose itself, free to act decisively and authentically, and so able to become who it is. It is this embeddedness in the possibility that today, at any moment, death could terminate all my possibilities – this affirmation of the inescapable fragility of all my options and commitments – that can make the difference between a stance towards death that fosters procrastination and a stance towards death that can overcome it.

Let's take a break from theorizing and turn to how, in actual stories, uncompromising confrontation with the reality of death – staring it in the face, right now – can bring us back to life with entirely new and unjaded verve. There is enough testimony of individuals being forcibly faced with this reality to fill whole libraries; here is just one, that of music journalist Tim Jonze, whose 'world came crashing down' when, only in his thirties, he was told he might have months to live after a shock diagnosis of acute myeloid leukaemia:

> It was time, I realized, to start living. A second bone marrow biopsy, performed at the end of 2018, showed no significant changes for the worse in my disease. And so, with my newfound appreciation of the ticking clock that beats inside all of us, cancer or no cancer, I really did start living. I threw myself into work, took up running again (smashing my pre-cancer personal bests just to prove I could) and absorbed huge joy in every tiny stupid thing: supermarket trips, the nursery run, edging the lawn. A visit to soft play now feels like paradise. Helen Jane got pregnant again, and this time it was neither twins nor a miscarriage. Nine months later, we welcomed Teddy into the world, our miracle baby who is loud and hilarious and able to get away with waking up at 4 a.m. every morning on account of the fact he looks like a baby red panda.
>
> I am now doing what I once thought was unthinkable: living happily with a chronic, incurable blood cancer. In a way, I am living happier because I have a chronic, incurable blood cancer.[3]

If huge joy can be had in a routine supermarket trip then surely all the more joy can be found in pursuing a priority that one sees as central to the meaning of one's life, and which one has the extraordinarily good fortune to possess the talents and resources to pursue.

Such testimony to the revitalizing power that can be found through facing death head-on in the midst of life – to how close encounter with its brute reality can return us to living with a force that we've never previously experienced – exists not just in the autobiography of individuals but also in those archetypal narratives that we call 'myth'. Far from depicting things that don't happen to ordinary mortals, myths are often the very opposite: ways of giving voice to fundamental structures of human experience that seem to apply to all people at all times and in all cultures – precisely by virtue of their being human and therefore inevitably death-bound. Whether or not the particular events they recount actually occurred hardly matters.

Homer's *Odyssey*, one of the founding texts of Western cultures, thought to have been composed in the eighth century BCE, describes the tumultuous sea journey of Odysseus, king of Ithaca and hero of the Trojan Wars, back to his homeland and to his wife Penelope. It's a journey that takes him ten years, during which time he repeatedly runs into dangers that threaten destruction and death, among them ominous monsters, like the one-eyed Cyclops or Scylla and Charybdis; storms and giants that pulverize the hardiest ships; cruel and all but invincible immortals, like the goddess Circe; the Sirens, who lure passers-by to death with their mesmerizing words and sweet songs; and the vengeful god of the sea, Poseidon.

Entertained for one year by the seductive and deceitful deity Circe – who can transform humans into animals and who tries to turn Odysseus into a pig so she can keep him for herself – he's finally reminded by his crew that he must leave:

[M]y loyal comrades took me aside and prodded,
'Captain, this is madness!
High time you thought of your own home at last,

if it really is your fate to make it back alive
and reach your well-built house and native land.'⁴

Though Circe has plied him with sex, food, and wine, none of which he resisted, he will not be detained. Pining for his home and family, he begs Circe to let him go:

My heart longs to be home,
my comrades' hearts as well. They wear me down,
pleading with me whenever you're away.

Eventually Circe does release him. But before he can head for Ithaca, she tells him, he needs to have a rendezvous with the dead. What she has in mind is not merely an 'acceptance of mortality', or the inevitability that we're all going to die, but a much more direct contending with the reality of death. He needs to descend to Hades, the land of the shades. There he will find wisdom in the person of the blind seer Tiresias – wisdom he needs to return to the world, charged with new power to live life:

[A]nother journey calls. You must travel down
to the House of Death and the awesome one,
   Persephone,
there to consult the ghost of Tiresias, seer of
   Thebes,
the great blind prophet whose mind remains
   unshaken.
Even in death – Persephone has given him wisdom,
everlasting vision to him and him alone . . .
the rest of the dead are empty, flitting shades.

Shattered by this news, Odysseus relays Circe's order to his crew:

> You think we are headed home, our own dear land?
> Well, Circe sets us a rather different course . . .
> down to the House of Death and the awesome one,
>   Persephone,
> there to consult the ghost of Tiresias, seer of
>   Thebes.

And he continues:

> Back to the swift ship at the water's edge we went,
> our spirits deep in anguish, faces wet with tears.

Enveloped in Hades, with its 'endless, deadly night', this intrepid hero of Greek myth is overcome by the emotion least known to him: fear. 'The dead,' he says, 'came surging round me, hordes of them, thousands raising unearthly cries, and blanching terror gripped me – panicked now that Queen Persephone might send up from Death some monstrous head, some Gorgon's staring face!'[5]

Here in the underworld, in search of the wisdom of Tiresias, Odysseus is encircled by the fate that we will all meet. He is compelled to look directly at the other side of life without being able to turn away or to euphemize it into a distant abstraction. And the shades he stumbles upon there leave him in no doubt about its horrors. The greatest hero of the ancient world, Achilles, laments that Hades is a realm without joy; that he would choose even the most menial form of life, as the slave of a pauper, over being king of all the dead. Nor is Achilles the only one Odysseus recognizes.

He shudders when he sees his own mother, who, he discovers only now, has died pining for him during his long absence.

For all its horror, the Greeks of the epic and classical ages regarded such an immediate encounter with death as a path to blessedness, making possible a return to life with entirely fresh clarity of insight and purpose. Their name for this revitalizing descent to Hades is *katabasis*, literally a 'going down'. Its moral is that unflinchingly to confront death, where all hope, help, and possibility are annihilated, nourishes an intimacy with life and an intoxication with it that can be found in no other way. Indeed, it is often the precondition for discovering and attaining our real aims. For this reason, many heroes of the later Roman and medieval worlds also undertake such a journey. In Virgil's *Aeneid*, composed between about 30 and 19 BCE, the hero Aeneas only learns of his destiny to found Rome when he descends to the underworld. Dante's journey to the divine presence, as he tells it over thirteen centuries later, must pass through various levels of hell and must witness the fate of many of the dead as essential stages on his journey to supreme blessedness.

Ancient heroes, such as Odysseus, and the incurably ill of our time, such as Tim Jonze, find themselves compelled into a proximity to death, precisely as an immediately present possibility, that is denied to the rest of us. We cannot get so close, not with the greatest empathy or the most vivid imagination in the world – crucial though both empathy and imagination are to confronting ourselves with our mortality. But if we wish to return to our own life with fresh clarity of purpose and renewed energy to pursue our highest priorities then we must strive to follow their example. In other words, we must resolutely anticipate our own death – not least by allowing the deaths of others, especially loved ones, to fill us with their reality, rather than reflexively consigning them to the shadows. And, in our stance towards life, we must come face to face, as best we can, with the extinguishing of our own existence, which can assail us at any time.

6

Embrace the Spirit of Play

What if we cannot overcome procrastination by lowering the stakes of our highest priorities in the ways I've suggested: reimagining them as escapes into less pressing tasks; worrying less about future rewards that we hope to reap from them, above all the recognition of our contemporaries and the good opinion of posterity; and avoiding the mirage of perfection? What, too, if raising their stakes through manoeuvring ourselves into intimacy with the ever-present possibility of our own death doesn't suffice to unleash our motivation? So that although we've jolted ourselves into action we still can't sustain it.

How, then, do we keep going?

This is where the spirit of play comes in – perhaps the most durable, because pleasurable, of all antidotes to procrastination.

By 'play' I don't mean that we need to slow down, work less, dispense with rules and discipline, or abandon a tight focus on our life priorities and purposes. Rather, I mean a different manner of working to that fostered by the cult of work, with its soul-destroying spirit of productivity, targets and deadlines. In contrast, play is that explorative and often joyful mindset by which we loosen, again through an effort of imagination, the paralysed cogs of our mind, releasing it from the managerial dullness and rigidity of the to-do list mentality and allowing it to move nimbly. It's a mindset in which we conjure a sense of freedom in the pursuit of our priorities, but not in which we seek to escape them. It's a way of stepping outside ordinary everyday routine in order to give ourselves better control over ordinary everyday routine.

In the film *Groundhog Day* (1993), Phil Connors, an obnoxious TV weatherman played by Bill Murray, discovers a way out of a life trapped in repetitiveness and routine, not by seeking to escape it but, on the contrary, by engaging with it in an entirely new way – a way redolent of just this spirit of play. He's been assigned to report on the annual Groundhog Day holiday in a small Pennsylvania town called Punxsutawney, together with his producer, Rita, played by Andie MacDowell. He dislikes everything about the job – the locals, the Groundhog ritual, the town itself – and is impatient to get it over with so that he can leave as quickly as possible. Infuriatingly for him, though, a blizzard traps him for the night. Worse is to follow. Awakening the following morning, he finds that it's Groundhog Day, 2 February, yet again – although not for others around him, for whom it's the next day, as usual. Phil discovers that he's compelled to live this very same day, not once, not twice, not three times, but on an open-ended time loop (it's ten thousand years in the original screenplay by Danny Rubin), including waking each morning to the same song, Sonny and Cher's 'I Got You, Babe'.

In despair, he resorts to drink. Sitting in a bowling alley with a couple of drunks from town, he asks them, 'What would you do if you were stuck in one place, and every day was exactly the same, and nothing that you did mattered?'

(the experience, we could add, of many trapped in dreary jobs or relationships or chores). Their answer is to do whatever you feel like. See what gives you kicks, they suggest. It would be easy to enjoy any number of passing pleasures because there'd be no lasting consequences to whatever you did. After all, Phil would start every day with a clean slate.

He's persuaded. Desperate to numb himself to his horrific monotony, he provokes a car chase with police, which leads to him being arrested and imprisoned; he indulges in numerous one-night stands; he gets into robberies; he gorges himself on cake regardless of the consequences for his health. Then he tries to seduce Rita – repeatedly and each time unsuccessfully. Feeling that none of these random thrills is leading anywhere, his thoughts turn to suicide. But suicide is impossible because he's going to awake again the next morning, on Groundhog Day, whatever he does. Confiding his fate to Rita, she persuades him to transform his perspective from cynical passivity to imaginative creativity, and from self-centredness to care for others – so that from the prison of identical circumstances he may keep reinventing himself. 'Maybe it's not a curse,' she tells him. 'Maybe it depends on how you look at it.' Through her, he comes to see novel opportunities to explore better ways of living the single day to which he's been condemned. He acquires fresh knowledge and skills; he takes risks on behalf of worthwhile aims that previously he would have shunned; he befriends local people, opening himself to their unique lives and needs, and, as a result, forging deeper relationships than he has ever known. He learns to play the piano, to speak French, to sculpt ice. He saves a boy from breaking his leg and throws himself into other good deeds, notably showing deep compassion to a homeless old man. Not least, he finds himself falling in love with Rita rather than merely wanting to sleep with her – and, as his transformation gathers pace and she witnesses his virtuosic piano playing, his newly inspiring TV reports, and his good deeds, so too does she with him. He declares his love to her and they spend the night together. The next morning Phil wakes up and finds that time has finally moved on: it's 3 February.

Groundhog Day is a powerful redemption story evoking the potential of each one of us, even where we're condemned to endlessly repetitive tasks, to wrest creativity from the mundane, novelty from sameness, and unfamiliarity from the familiar. It's reminiscent of a test, posed by Nietzsche, of our ability to affirm the life we have, including all its tedium and suffering, all its disappointments and failures. The test is how we would respond if a devil were to tell us that our entire life is fated to recur identically in every respect an infinite number of times. Would we fall into despair at this prospect? Or would we rather welcome it – indeed '*crave nothing more fervently*', as Nietzsche puts it – out of an overwhelming love of life, regardless of what it brings us? To give the second answer – to welcome the eternal recurrence of the life we have, down to its every detail – is, he holds, the 'highest formula of affirmation' that is possible.[1]

Phil's test might be even harder than Nietzsche's because we're told that Phil explicitly remembers every one of the time loops he relives; Nietzsche, on the other hand, leaves open the question whether anyone *could* remember their previously occurring lives. After all, if, as in Nietzsche's test, every recurrence is identical, down to its smallest detail, how could we distinguish any particular recurrence from any other? And so how could we even know that we're stuck on a time loop? Moreover, Phil is fated to repeat only a single calendar day rather than the richness of a whole life. But the lessons of Phil's situation and Nietzsche's thought experiment are the same: the perspective we have on our life can dramatically transform it from cynical negation to inspired joy, from a nightmare of tedium to endless opportunities for delight.

Which brings us back to play. It's clear that play in the sense that Phil comes to exemplify it, and as I mean it here, is precisely not about fleeing the everyday. Nor is it about making things easy – as the term 'child's play' can suggest. It isn't to mess around irresponsibly or pretend that we're kids without a worry in the world. Least of all is it a life of licence, bereft of purpose or consequence – the kind of life that Phil first tries as a way of coping with imprisonment in the time loop. On the contrary, play is an 'existential' mood – a spirit, a mindset, a stance towards the world – that transforms our entire way of experiencing almost any task. It experiments with new ways forward for our projects: ways of engaging more deeply with the reality in which we find ourselves; ways that are always tentative and never allowed to become tyrannical over us, bogging us down in stale routine. Sensing, for example, a dead end in how we've been pursuing a goal, we withdraw from the attempt, not with a sense of failure but out of the pleasure of having tried one path and now exploring another. Still failing to see a clear way forward, and still bogged down, we might even return to our starting point, toying with a fresh way of inhabiting it.

In this sense, we could approach almost everything we do in the spirit of play, from work to relationships to leisure and even to sadder, weightier tasks, such as caring for an unwell elderly parent. Indeed, it dissolves borders that we traditionally construct between, say, work and leisure, or what lies within our control and what doesn't.

Although we might think that play is necessarily free of purposes or goals – that the whole point of it is to explore and enjoy without being tethered to ends – this manifestly isn't the case. Purpose is often at the heart of playing, even when we are 'lost' in experimental play. In the case of games, for example a tennis match, the purpose is to excel at the skills they demand and to gain the satisfaction of winning. For a pianist, playful experimentation might be motivated by the search for a beautiful musical phrase or the spirit that must structure a whole piece. Two people who are passionately attracted to one another will enjoy frolicking, teasing, touching, and banter not only for its own sake – not only without purpose – but also as foreplay that consciously anticipates deeper pleasure and intimacy.

Such purposiveness is true, too, for children absorbed in play. One only need observe their fierce concentration to notice how guided by ends their play can be; how serious their intent is. We can see how the child – playing, for example, with its puppet theatre – is palpably conjuring a world by experimenting with the puppet forms it finds at its disposal, ordering and reordering them to explore its own temperament, desires, and skills. Even kicking a ball against a wall isn't necessarily without purpose, which might be to discover and enjoy one's strength; to delight in the sensory pleasure of the ball smacking against a resistance and ricocheting; to practise for a contest with a competitor. Sigmund Freud beautifully expresses the power of children's play to creatively order and enjoy their world, including its ends, when he says:

Might we not say that every child at play behaves like a creative writer, in that he creates a world of his own, or rather, rearranges the things of his world in a new way which pleases him? It would be wrong to think he does not take that world seriously; on the contrary, he takes his play very seriously and he expends large amounts of emotion on it.[2]

Nietzsche goes further and – in the way that I am suggesting here – asks us to see adult life in precisely such terms, as a child immersed seriously in play. In one of his provocative asides, he even claims that the true 'maturity' of an adult 'consists in having found again the seriousness one had as a child, at play'. The child, Nietzsche says, 'is innocence and forgetting, a new beginning, a game, a self-propelled wheel, a first movement, a sacred "Yes"'.[3]

A game. A new beginning. A sacred yes. Nietzsche's vision of maturity and creativity as play takes us, once again, back to ancient Greek thought, where the image of the child at play is employed to evoke the flourishing human life (and even the nature of the cosmos). The sage Heraclitus, who flourished in the fifth century BCE and who left only riddling fragments, enigmatically said of the *aiōn*, variously translated as 'vitality', 'a human lifetime', 'eternity', or 'time' itself: 'Lifetime is a child at play, moving pieces in a game. Kingship belongs to the child.'[4] If kingship belongs to the child, this suggests that precisely what procrastination loses – a sovereign sense of control over one's life, of creative ordering, of pursuing one's priorities in the way and at the tempo one wishes – can be secured by play.

Intriguingly, in Greek the words for 'to play' (*paizein*) and 'child' (*pais*) are etymologically related, suggesting that if the successful life is play then the model for it is indeed a child at play. Moreover, 'to play' (*paizein*) is also related to *paideia*, which denotes, variously, 'education' or 'culture'. Which, according to the classical scholar Armand D'Angour, reflects the reality that in ancient Greece the connections between play and such achievements of high culture as art and literature are 'insistent and inescapable'. And he speculates that 'the centrality of forms of play in Greek culture has seemed to offer a clue to its enduring intellectual and artistic accomplishments'.[5]

Plato adds his own profound twist to this thought. 'What, then, is the right way of living?' he asks. And he answers: 'Life must be lived as play, playing certain games, making sacrifices, singing and dancing, and then a person will be able to propitiate the gods, and defend himself against his enemies, and *win in the contest*.'[6]

Will be able to propitiate the gods. Will be able to defend himself against his enemies. Will be able to win in the contest. Clearly, in this passage Plato, too, sees play as fundamentally purposive; and, moreover, as directed at, and central to, three of the most crucial goals of life for the Greeks of his times. Play here is anything but the meandering of the slothful or the random darting around of the distracted. Indeed, Plato emphasizes, play is what the gods *want humans to do*. Humanity should 'play the noblest games and be of another mind from what they are at present'. Its aims are therefore nothing if not directed at supreme priorities and nothing if not serious.

In modern times this ancient relation of play to culture has been taken up more broadly in a brilliant treatise, *Homo ludens*, published by the historian Johan Huizinga in 1938. The very title of Huizinga's book characterizes humanity not as the wise species – *sapiens* – but as the playful species – *ludens*. Crucially, for Huizinga as for Plato, play is not a frivolous pastime, but is instead fundamental to the origin of almost all human culture. It is, he argues, nothing less than the root of law and order, commerce and profit, craft and art, poetry, wisdom and science. All of these, he says, are 'rooted in the primeval soil of play'. To a great extent, he argues, '*culture itself* bears the character of play'. Indeed, civilization 'arises *in* and *as* play, and never leaves it'.[7]

Huizinga is deeply convinced that, as the root of those achievements, from law and order to art and poetry, play is necessarily rule-based. In a striking definition, he says that play

> is an activity which proceeds within certain limits of time and space, in a visible order, according to rules freely accepted, and outside the sphere of necessity or material utility. The play-mood is one of rapture and enthusiasm, and is sacred or festive in accordance with the occasion. A feeling of exaltation and tension accompanies the action.[8]

Being rule-based, play 'creates order, *is* order. Into an imperfect world and into the confusion of life it brings a temporary, a limited perfection'.[9] It is precisely this power to create order, to establish rules and conventions, that leads Huizinga to see play as fundamental to the constitution of all community – and of civilization itself. Thus, when we speak of 'fair play', we're speaking of members of a community – equally and with the consideration due to each other – abiding by its rules, whether those rules are explicitly formulated or implicitly accepted. 'To play by the rules' is an unbreakable condition of their membership in the whole.

We don't need to accept in its entirety Huizinga's claim that play is fundamental to the origin of human cultures to see it as an existential attitude – a way of being – that steps out of the habitual in order to approach our priorities with a fresh spirit; one of joyful experimentation. This spirit is very different to the cult of autonomy, which is so often understood as promising that, like flicking a switch, we can choose to do what we like, when we like, and to the extent we like; where all the emphasis is on our imperialistic, untrammelled agency. In place of this ethos of command and control, play inspires an attitude of submission to our projects and of following our imagination where it takes us. Similarly, it subverts the grim seriousness of the cult of work, so that thinking becomes less tethered to process and routine. We become open to new ways forward, new ideas, surprise.

This has been borne out in countless innovations, from the seemingly mundane to the greatest leaps in medicine and science. In his book *Wonderland: How Play Made the Modern World*, Steven Johnson shows how such modern advances as artificial intelligence, the digital revolution, probability theory and (out of the latter) even the insurance industry, stem – in a line of influence and inspiration that can stretch back centuries – from eccentrics delightedly experimenting for the pleasure of it, often in their own homes. In ninth-century Baghdad, for example, three brothers, now known as the Banū [sons of] Mūsà bin Shākir, working in the House of Wisdom, a place dedicated to Islamic scholarship and innovation, developed engineering tools that were far ahead of their times, such as crankshafts and twin-cylinder pumps with suction, which they collected in a book called *Kitāb al-hiyal, The Book of Ingenious Devices*, published around 850 CE. One of their successors, an even more prolific engineer and polymath called Ismail al-Jazari (1136–1206 CE), described a further series of astounding developments, such as 'float valves that prefigure the design of modern toilets [and] flow regulators that would eventually be used in hydroelectric dams and internal combustion engines'. These, along with hundreds of other inventions, were collected by al-Jazari, sometimes known as the father of modern robotics, in a richly illustrated work, *Kitāb fī ma 'rifat al-hiyal al-handasiyya, The Book of Knowledge of Ingenious Mechanical Devices*, published in 1206.[10] According to its English translator, Donald Hill,

> it is impossible to overemphasize the importance of al-Jazari's work in the history of engineering. Until modern times there is no other document from any cultural area that provides a comparable wealth of instructions for the design, manufacture, and assembly of machines ... The impact of al-Jazari's inventions is still felt in contemporary mechanical engineering.[11]

Strikingly, both these volumes were filled with designs for playful objects like 'fountains that spout water in rhythmic bursts; mechanical flute players; automated drumming machines; a peacock that dispenses water when you pull its feather and then proffers a miniature servant with soap; [and] a boat filled with robotic musicians that can serenade an audience while floating in a lake'.[12] At the heart of these curiosities were technological feats that would appear in Europe and America only centuries later, inspiring maverick geniuses in the mould of the Banū Mūsà brothers and al-Jazari, and in turn contributing to the vast cultural transformations spawned by industrialization. For example, the idea of a programmable machine traces a line, direct and indirect, to the walking, quacking, and waddling mechanical duck designed by an eighteenth-century eccentric named Jacques de Vaucanson (the most notorious gimmick of which was that it could take in food and subsequently defecate).[13] Vaucanson was, in turn, followed by the remarkable Charles Babbage – a nineteenth-century inventor and writer – whose childhood memory of being shown an automated doll, capable of uncannily human-like movements, in the attic of another experimenter called John-Joseph Merlin inspired his path-breaking invention of the calculating machine.[14] Arguably the first programmable computer ever imagined, Babbage's machine augured the explosion of computing power in the late twentieth century and of the IT and AI revolutions that are still unfolding. The most 'serious' fields, like computing and automation, can be catalysed by the weirdest contraptions and the most bizarre obsessions.

As Steven Johnson notes, entrepreneurs might have made fortunes out of the idea of programmability, but 'it was the artists and illusionists who brought the idea into the world in the first place'[15] – people like the Banū Mūsà brothers and al-Jazari, through Vaucanson to Merlin, Babbage, and many others. Nor, of course, has the power of play to innovate been lost on contemporary businesses of all stripes. In the hope of inspiring new products, companies as diverse as Google and Lego, Pixar, Nvidia, and 3M, cultivate an environment of free-wheeling playfulness and exploration, often ring-fencing a proportion of employees' work time for projects of their choosing in dedicated spaces. And, as such companies amply confirm, the spirit of play is in no way inconsistent with the competitive will to win, let alone with purpose-driven thinking. On the contrary, as Plato already held, the very aim of play can be to 'win in the contest'. Play doesn't entail curtailing ambition for the sake of a more chillaxed life. It isn't a synonym for staying in the moment and resisting all focus on what lies beyond. Least of all is it a prescription for passing the time in random doodling, pleasant and therapeutic though that can be. Rather, it can be deeply purposive, ambitious, focused, serious, and even urgent in its priorities, while pursuing them in a spirit of joyful experimentation. In this way it can free us from the deadlock, the staleness, the sense of slavery to cold process and productivity that lie at the heart of so much procrastination.

7
Harness the Power of Regret

No feeling is more abundantly created by procrastination than regret – along with its closely allied emotions, shame and remorse. Regret over lost time, over impotent ambition, over betraying one's talents and cherished aims. Regret over disappointing the expectations of others and losing their respect. All this can corrode our self-esteem, miring us in despair and threatening our selfhood.

And yet, as we'll see, regret is far from being an entirely negative emotion. It can also force us to notice that we're on the wrong path and to correct course. It can be salvational.

Regret bites especially hard in our modern era with its cults of autonomy and work, which besiege us with extravagant but often disappointed expectations that we can – and should – sovereignly choose our ends in life and then implement them through a stream of recognized achievements. In pre-modern times, when the goals of life were seen as largely given by divine ordinance, or by tradition, ancestors, or nature, regret about falling short of those goals was already among the most powerful, even brutal, of emotions. But today, when we each see ourselves as a self-constructed and self-endorsed work in progress, we can regret not only our failure to implement our priorities but those priorities themselves. And to that extent we can regret the very self – the very identity – that we've constructed. So when my agency fails and I just can't make progress with my projects, and my time flows away to no useful purpose, this double-headed monster of regret makes me feel a failure in regard to both my choices (or lack of them) *and* my ability to realize them.

In this aloneness with my despair, I naturally ask myself the what-if question: 'What if there's a more motivating and exciting project to work on?' 'Or a project that the world offers me more opportunity to pursue?' 'What if I've missed my true vocation?' 'What if I'd married my college sweetheart, who I now realize would have been the Right One, and with whom I'd have flourished instead of sitting here stuck on my own or with a boring spouse?' 'What if I'd had the courage to lobby for that promotion, like the guy who got it despite being so much less qualified than I am?' I tell myself that if only I'd taken those paths, everything about my life would now be better; I'd be inspired and driven, and this horrible urge to escape my situation – to procrastinate over my actual choices – would be overcome.

The nagging seductiveness of what might have been, or what might still be, isn't only a *result* of procrastinating over the priorities I've chosen; a way of escaping the pain of procrastination and all its resulting regrets. Once fantasizing about the what-if life gets going, it, in turn, can become a potent *cause* of further procrastination over those priorities as the pleasures and benefits of alternative paths come to shine more vividly than anything about my stalled, energy-sapping current life. And the more vividly they shine so the more what-if imaginings turn into if-only yearnings – tempting me to cut my losses now and seek new pastures.

The often perilous seductiveness of the what-if/if-only

life is underscored by the psychoanalyst and essayist Adam Phillips, who proposes that 'sometimes – perhaps more often than not – we think we know more about the experiences we don't have than about the experiences that we do have, "frustration" being our word for the experience of not having an experience'. 'In our unlived lives', he adds, 'we are always more satisfied, far less frustrated versions of ourselves'. Indeed, our wishes for those other lived lives enable us to 'bridge the gap between what we are and what we want to be as if by magic'.[1]

The experiences we don't have aren't more alluring just because we choose to see their advantages and ignore their drawbacks. Beyond that, Phillips appears to suggest, they seem more real, more attainable, and more familiar in the demands they make on us than everything with which we're currently struggling. And he offers a motive for their allure: 'Our fantasies of satisfaction – our preconceptions about satisfaction – are where we hide from the possibility of real satisfaction', he writes.[2] Imagining alternative lives, in other words, is how we avoid the life we actually want to have. The life expressed by our treasured priorities.

But why would we want to hide from the possibility of real satisfaction?

I think the answer is this: because pursuing it – like pursuing almost anything real – involves risks, skills, sustained energy, and other demands that we fear (often of course groundlessly) we might not be up to. We dread putting our real self to the test, and we dread failure. As a result we procrastinate over our actual priorities, and instead lunge into fantasy satisfactions that we will, in practice, never act on. We might even justify our procrastination by convincing ourselves that the priority we're avoiding will anyway never come good for us, so there's no point persisting with it. Which will give us, at least, the pleasure of certainty – a pleasure never to be underrated! The relationship we're in, the project we're working on, the town we're living in, the organization we're employed by, the profession we've chosen, isn't going to work out, and this will never change. So let's move on to that other relationship or project or place that might be a better fit, and where we visualize a banquet of delights within easier reach. In the if-only life, the best party is always elsewhere.

Such regret-fuelled defeatism is, of course, self-fulfilling. It might give us the pleasure of certainty and avoid the risk of trying and failing, but its dangers couldn't be starker. Rejection of the ends to which we take ourselves to be most committed. A resort to magical thinking in order to skirt our actual priorities and the real satisfactions they offer. Further anguished regret when we realize that we've perfected the artistry of evasion at the cost of sabotaging our own life.

But regret at procrastinating can also have a very different – and very creative – outcome. It can be crucial to understanding who we are and therefore to becoming ourselves. Precisely because it's so hard to ignore, it can propel us back to our real priorities with fresh determination. Or, by contrast, it can send a powerful signal that they're in fact the wrong ones for us: neither meaningful nor conducive to our flourishing. And that sticking to them – to our existing vocations, projects, relationships – through thick and thin, doubling down on them because we can't face cutting our losses and moving on, isn't always the right choice. In these ways regret helps us to discover *from experience* what we really care about, and so to address the question that Socrates, Plato's great teacher, asks each of us as individuals: what does it mean to live a good life?

One of the earliest philosophers to explore how regret might give us the self-understanding to overcome procrastination was Plato's student, Aristotle. The word he and Plato use for acting in defiance of what we take to be best for us – for knowingly pursuing ends that contradict priorities to which we're committed – is *akrasia*; and, he insists, 'every akratic person is liable to regret'.[3]

According to the classical scholar James Warren, Aristotle sees regret – and its related emotion, remorse (both emotions denoted by the Greek word *metameleia*) – as necessarily delayed. Regret doesn't strike at the same time as we're consciously sabotaging the priority in question, and therefore acting against our better judgement. It is, Warren argues, a 'retrospective attitude of self-chastisement' that enables us to look back at a past action, to see what got in the way of pursuing our best interests, and so to correct how we act in the future out of what Aristotle calls 'anticipatory pain' at the thought of the consequences of our self-sabotaging behaviour.[4] Here Aristotle evokes one of the central experiences of procrastination: immediate pleasure in succumbing to our present desires but deferred pain at the damage we will do to our future self as a result.

But what does Aristotle regard as the exact target of the procrastinator's regret? Not only, it seems, our neglect of our real priorities. Regret is also aimed, quite specifically, at our positive motivation to succumb to the pleasures that have overridden and diverted us from those priorities. And such regret, he warns, can go all the way to extreme self-loathing.

It's at this point that his account gets really interesting. For in his relentless way, Aristotle probes at what exactly makes us decide to act against our best interests in the moment of procrastination. What, for example, happens when the impulse to smoke a cigarette that I know to be bad for me overrides my longer-term and deeper desire to protect my health?

What happens, he suggests, is a failure to *really* understand the consequences of succumbing to the short-term pleasurable distraction at the moment that we do so.[5] We might think we understand that an unhealthy lifestyle is bad for us and could end up imperiling our most cherished long-term aims. But, it seems Aristotle is saying, we haven't sufficiently internalized that it's bad and why it's bad. We don't vividly see, before our mind's eye, the implications of living unhealthily. We have a general rule in mind, such as 'smoking is dangerous', but we're only applying it vaguely to our own concrete situation. In essence, he says, we're acting ignorantly. For, paraphrasing Aristotle, to really know is for that knowledge to be effective in driving decision and action, rather than merely rote.

Aristotle illustrates this distinction between effective and rote knowledge by likening the latter to the state of being asleep or drunk. If you ask a drunk driver whether they know that they should stop at a red traffic light or observe the speed limit, they'll probably say that of course they do. What a patronizing question to ask them! But if they're severely inebriated then their knowledge will be no more effective at directing their actual behaviour than that of a small child, who also answers correctly but cannot be said to grasp the full significance of what they're saying. The drunk adult can parrot the rules, and they can be somehow aware that flouting them carries dangers, but they aren't seized of their true importance. And since their knowledge has so little purchase over their actions, they will be easily swayed by passing passions and pleasures. Thus, people under the influence of intense anger or sexual desire, Aristotle remarks,

> might utter scientific proofs or recite the poems of Empedocles, but they do not understand what they are saying. Beginners at a subject can put together the sentences, but they do not yet know the subject – it has to become part of themselves, and that takes time. We must therefore take what people say when they are acting akratically [or procrastinating] in the way we take what actors on a stage say.[6]

Although Aristotle seems manifestly unfair to actors who succeed in becoming their roles, for our purposes the key takeaway from his discussion of akrasia is that regret is only effective in getting us to change course if it drives us to intimately understand why acting contrary to our own declared priorities undermines our flourishing. As he shows, such understanding is very hard. Even the simple case of smoking that extra cigarette that I say I know is bad for me readily illustrates the difficulties. Do I really know what its long-term effects will likely be – if only in just factual terms that I can parrot, rather than as understanding that I've deeply internalized? And even if I do, this knowledge will come from studies of numerous other human beings. I'm aware that some people smoke all their lives and never get sick as a result while others who never smoke end up with lung cancer. In reality, I have little or no idea how the extra cigarette is going to affect *me*.

Our understanding of what we want and of the risks of acting contrary to it might almost always be murky. It becomes murkier still on one powerful contemporary image of the mind, which was unavailable to Aristotle, according to which our priorities – and our inhibitions to pursuing them – are deeply influenced by our vast unconscious life. But he does show that the pain of regret can be crucial in motivating us to seek such understanding. And that the way regret does this is by focusing us, with a power that no other emotion affords, on the cost – as best we can assess and grasp it – of avoiding or acting against those priorities, so that we might overcome our urge to do so.

Another picture of how regret can guide us to overcome procrastination and indeed show us definitively where our true priorities lie can be derived from the life and thought of the nineteenth-century Danish philosopher Søren Kierkegaard (1813–55). One of history's great amorous procrastinators, Kierkegaard describes how regret pulls him in opposite directions on one of the key decisions of his life: whether or not to marry. He discovers that he will regret it if he marries and he will regret it if he doesn't. Either way, he will lament the options that each path must close off. Gradually, if painfully, regret affords him deeper insight into what is gained and lost in following these paths, and above all into who he is. His struggle is eventually resolved in what he describes as one of those moments of 'unshakable sureness in oneself' when 'a strange illumination spreads over life – without [our] needing in even the remotest manner to understand all particulars'.[7] This is the kind of moment, he suggests some years later, when we look back over our life and – only now, with the benefit of hindsight – can begin to understand what we've done and why we've done it. For, he insists, in a memorable insight, although life 'must be lived forwards' it can only be 'understood backwards'.[8]

The boyfriend, suitor, and fiancé from hell, in May 1837, aged twenty-four, Kierkegaard meets a fifteen-year-old girl called Regine Olsen, whom he assiduously courts for the next three years. But no sooner is he launched on his mission of securing the hand in marriage of, as he puts it, 'my heart's sovereign mistress' and 'unknown divinity' than he hesitates. On the one hand, he breathlessly serenades her – to her face and in the privacy of his journal:

> Everywhere, in every girl's face, I see features of your beauty, yet I think that I'd need all the girls in the world to extract, as it were, your beauty from theirs, that I'd have to crisscross the whole world to find the continent I lack yet . . . which the deepest secret of my whole 'I' magnetically points to – and the next moment you are so near me, so present, so richly supplementing my spirit that I am transfigured.[9]

On the other hand, as the Kierkegaard scholar David Hannay argues, his diary entries over the period 1837–40 'betray an increasing anxiety':

> Should he take his theology finals, finish his thesis, and get a job? Perhaps propose to Regine and 'realize the universal' [i.e. a conventional way of life, with its socially mandated responsibilities, duties, and values] by becoming husband, priest, or teacher? But what then of this budding talent as writer? Being a writer

takes time and concentration, and the talent has to be proved. But then again one cannot just be a writer – there must be a life-view [that one's vocation serves]. But what if the life-view says you should marry and get a job? What happens then to the writing?[10]

All this hesitation notwithstanding, Kierkegaard continues to woo Regine passionately but erratically. Until, on 8 September 1840, he proposes to her in her parents' house. In another journal entry he describes the scene:

> There we stood, the two of us alone in the living room. She was a little flustered. I asked her to play something for me as she usually did. She does so but I don't manage to say anything. Then I suddenly grab the score, close it not without a certain vehemence, throw it onto the piano and say: 'Oh! What do I care for music, it's you I want, I have wanted you for two years.' She kept silent. As it happens, I had taken no steps to persuade her, I had even warned her against me, against my melancholy. And when she mentioned a relationship with Schlegel [a rival suitor], I said: 'Let that relationship be a parenthesis for I have first priority.' She mostly kept silent.[11]

Two days later, she accepts. Almost immediately, he regrets his decision. Was he rash to propose? Is marriage really for him?

His panicking, exacerbated by depression, flummoxes and distresses the inexperienced Regine. As his intellectual biographer Clare Carlisle puts it, he develops a melancholia so intense that even his appearance is altered – so much so that just a few days after the engagement, when he and

Regine meet by chance on the street, she doesn't recognize him.[12]

Through all this agonizing, however, he sends her a steady stream of letters, often replete with passionate declarations, which we have no reason to believe aren't deeply felt:

> Know that every time you repeat that you love me from the deepest recesses of your soul, it is as though I heard it for the first time, and just as a man who owned the whole world would need a lifetime to survey his splendors, so I also seem to need a lifetime to contemplate all the riches contained in your love.[13]

And he assures her of the depth of his desire for her:

> If I dared to wish, then I certainly know what I would wish for. And that wish is identical with my deepest convictions: that [here Kierkegaard is quoting from Paul's letter to the Romans 8: 38–9] neither Death, nor Life, nor Principalities, nor Powers, nor the Present, nor that which is to come, nor the Exalted, nor the Profound, nor any other creature may tear me from you, or you from me.[14]

At the same time, tearing himself from Regine is precisely what he strives to do. Although deeply aware of the cruelty of his tortured ambivalence, his concerns about marriage and its duties and constraints refuse to abate. Finally, after a whole year of this, he concludes that the answer is no, and on 11 October 1841, plunging Regine into darkest despair, he breaks off the engagement, takes back the ring he gave her, and two weeks later flees to Berlin.

But the year of back-and-forth wanting and regretting, culminating in the termination of their relationship, is by no means the end of the great philosopher's indecisiveness. In his sojourn of nearly five months in Berlin he is repeatedly beset by images of her. So, too, on his next visit to the city, the following year, he imagines returning to her, and now regrets not the engagement but breaking it off: 'If I had had faith, I would have stayed with Regine', he confides to his journal on 17 May 1843.[15] And yet, as Clare Carlisle writes, tormented as his heart still is, 'all has been decided outwardly'. He has

> set his life in a different direction. He knows that he will never marry. When he sees Regine in church or on the street [after returning again to Copenhagen] – and he sees her often – he cannot speak to her. The image of her face and the echo of her final desperate words to him flood his soul with confused, conflicting feelings; all his thoughts of her are tangled with his effort to understand himself.[16]

Manipulative and cruel to Regine Kierkegaard certainly was; but it's also true that searing regret was crucial to making perhaps the hardest decision of his life: to forgo the woman he loved for his vocation as a writer – a vocation he came to believe was incompatible with the duties and responsibilities of marriage. Regret, by turns guilty and self-justifying – first at proposing to Regine and then at breaking off their engagement and forfeiting the happiness of conjugal life – forced him to the conviction that he couldn't genuinely live the life of both a philosopher-writer and a married man. What it takes – what it really means – to authentically be either of these things – writer or husband – rather than to fall into them in the fake, complacent, and socially correct way in which they are so often pursued, demands, he thought, an existential choice for one or the other, and the courage to follow the road that this choice might ordain. It's only in wholeheartedly making a choice *as the particular person one is*, and, as Kierkegaard puts it, 'born in this country, at this time, under the many-faceted influence of all these changing surroundings',[17] that one becomes a real person: a human being who is true to themselves and who lives in a truthful relation to the world.

If we avoid such existential choices – if we fudge them by trying to live two or more intensely demanding forms of life that are ultimately incompatible, under the illusion that we can have it all – we will never fully live. It won't even be true, for us, that, as the saying goes, 'we only live once'. And it's in impelling us to existential choices that regret can play such an essential role. With its clarifying pain – its tremendous power to make vivid to our mind's eye what we lose by pursuing one life priority over another – regret can bring the necessary decisions to a head, enabling us to go for one form of life, and to live it authentically and to the full. Which, in Kierkegaard's case, meant allowing regret to force into focus, on the one hand, what he felt would be lost by compromising the vocation of writer through choosing Regine and the married life, versus, on the other hand, what he would lose by saying no to Regine through choosing the lonely path of the writer.

There's only one other similarly agonizing emotion – or, more accurately perhaps, mood or state of being – that's also both a cause and an effect of procrastination, and that can also penetrate and permeate our inner world sufficiently to propel a far-reaching re-evaluation of our priorities and how we're pursuing them. Are they the right ones for me? If they're not, for what should I strive? If they are, am I pursuing them in the best way? Moreover, is the spirit in which I am approaching *anything* I value conducive to achieving it? This other emotion is boredom; and, like regret, it is, I suggest, one of the keys to overcoming procrastination.

8

Let Boredom Save Us

A new day. I've just got to my desk. I'm excited about returning to work on a project that grips me. I've completed my usual preparatory routine: a good night's sleep, thirty minutes of cardio workout, a shower, an ample but not a heavy breakfast, a coffee – then another coffee. Maddeningly, I can't start. I try to revive the thought I left off yesterday. But it's flat; dead on arrival. So I just start writing without knowing what I want to say, hoping that a stream of consciousness, or unconsciousness, will spill out onto the page. The book, of course, refuses to write itself. A few more attempts, each one more random than its predecessor. In the hope of stumbling on an inner reset button that will allow a fresh start, I allow myself a few light distractions. Read a couple of newspapers online. Snoop on the scandals and furies littering social media. Stimulate myself with some full-fat milk chocolate. But this makes me more restless still – and my focus more elusive. Overwhelmed by the tedium of all this stalemated effort, I find myself sliding into what I most dread: indifference, the numbing of motivation, and finally boredom.

What now?

The answer is that this is – it has to be – my opportunity to turn bored indifference to good use. To harness it – like regret – to overcoming procrastination. Which might sound like wishful thinking – one of those rote claims that all adversity can be turned to advantage. But it isn't because it's obviously absurd that I'm apathetic doing what I love doing and deeply believe in. And that I'm apathetic to the point where I'm sporadically severed from all contact with the project – where the whole thing becomes a nightmare. So I try this: I try to zero in on my boredom and to become as intimate as possible with it. Not to fight it – at least not yet – but to observe it, including the frantic urge to escape the task at hand that it engenders. I want to see what it's actually saying, or resisting, or wanting, or fleeing.

In this endeavour – to understand why I feel boredom when I try to evade a goal that I crave to pursue rather than merely something that I have no desire to do – I have a tremendous ally: a fourth-century monk, living in the Egyptian desert, called Evagrius of Pontus. Struck by how often his fellow monks became apathetic, even hostile, towards God and the life of prayer to which they had sworn allegiance, Evagrius wrote a whole treatise examining their experience, moment by moment. The puzzle that he wrestled with was the same one that guides this book: why do we avoid precisely what we see as the best possible life for us – a life to which we believe ourselves to be devoted? And how can we overcome this tremendous urge to escape our own, often intensely-felt, commitments?

For the monks, the best possible life was one dedicated to God through the concentration demanded by the monastic existence. They had pursued their calling out of deep conviction, sacrificing to it every other kind of life available at the time. Their problem was similar to what Plato and Aristotle had identified in their analysis of akrasia:

knowingly acting in defiance of what we take to be best for us. It seems that, although they never wavered in their conviction that the most rigorous devotion to God was the best life, they nonetheless yearned to escape it.

Evagrius's starting point was the inner restlessness that impelled a monk to abandon a monastic life to which he felt both personally pledged and called by God. Egged on by the 'noonday demon' – so called because the demon cunningly struck in the oppressive heat of midday, when the monks were at their most lethargic – the monk's restlessness was accompanied by a stifling sense of time dragging monotonously on. Interred in his solitude, he would begin to hate his vocation, casting around irritably for any diversion, any alternative path, that would offer him a way out. The word Evagrius used to describe this frantic avoidance of what one holds to be one's life's highest priority is *acedia* – derived from a Greek word that means 'not caring', a state closely related if not identical to indifference:

> The demon of *acedia*, also called the noonday demon, is the most oppressive of all the demons. He attacks the monk about the fourth hour [10 a.m.] and besieges his soul until the eighth hour [2 p.m.]. First of all, he makes it appear that the sun moves slowly or not at all, and that the day seems to be fifty hours long. Then he compels the monk to look constantly towards the windows; to jump out of the cell; to watch the sun to see how far it is from the ninth hour [3 p.m.]; to look this way and that . . . And further, he instils in him a dislike for the place and for his state of life itself . . . He leads him on to a desire for other places where he can easily find the wherewithal to meet his needs and

pursue a trade that is easier and more productive; he adds that pleasing the Lord is not a question of being in a particular place: for Scripture says that the divinity can be worshipped everywhere [John 4:21–4]. He joins to these suggestions the memory of his close relations and of his former life; he depicts for him the long course of his lifetime, while bringing the burdens of asceticism before his eyes; and, as the saying has it, he deploys every device in order to have the monk leave his cell and flee the stadium.[1]

The demon's real job here isn't to tempt the monks with specific alternative lives or a menu of possible distractions. It's to prime them to be restless, to be daunted by the idea of a lifetime dedicated to their demanding vocation, and to crave less arduous ways of pursuing it. Once primed in this way, they, like most of us procrastinators today, will find for themselves all the distractions they need.

Evagrius wasn't the last to explore the phenomenon of acedia in detail. Nearly a thousand years later, towards the close of Europe's long Middle Ages, Thomas Aquinas – the thirteenth-century philosopher and perhaps the most influential of all Christian thinkers – argued that acedia so sabotages our pursuit of good ends that it should be deemed one of the 'seven deadly sins': those sins that are destructive of all goodness and, in turn, the root cause of all other evils.

Thomas characterized acedia as flight from the most joyful life one could live; a flight grounded in an 'oppressive sorrow' that turns us away from all good deeds – and that even finds the good 'repugnant'.[2] For a medieval Christian the highest good remained God; devotion to this highest good was ordained by God, beginning with the command to love God with 'all your heart and all your soul and all your might' (Mark 12:30). Note *'all'*: devotion to God, to the ways of God, to the moral world order ordained by God, indeed to the entire order of existence created by God, wasn't merely experienced as the highest good among other good ends; it was the good that structured and gave purpose to all other good ends and the only conceivable way of understanding the purpose of existence – whether one was the most powerful monarch or the lowliest serf.

What is at stake with acedia that turns us away from God is therefore nothing less than rebellion against, or indifference to, created existence. Instead, we settle for a life that, in going against the order of the cosmos, is certain to come to grief. And to come to grief not just in this world but, in view of the divine justice inevitably meted out for such tremendous betrayal, in an eternity of damnation.

We don't need to share that view to profit from Thomas's investigation into the intense 'torpor of mind' that sabotages our own flourishing. For, he suggests, when such torpor pervades our whole being it doesn't merely evade good ends temporarily, so that we can return to them at any time of our choosing. Nor is its cost merely in lost time. Rather, it 'so depresses a man that he wants to do nothing'. Someone afflicted in this way 'cannot face getting down to work' – and, in particular, they are dragged 'away from good work'. They lose all joy in those beneficial things that should fill them with delight – foremost among which are love and charity, which Thomas sees as the essence of any relationship to our highest good.

Such a total loss of joy in love is, he implies, worse than seeing it as all too often fraudulent, deluded, and destructive. It's worse, too, than being so fearful of love's entanglements and vulnerabilities that we avoid the risk of engaging in it. We can be cynical about love's forgeries and/or fearful of its risk, and yet remain committed to it as an ideal. But if, under the influence of acedia, we become indifferent or hostile to it, we will dismiss love as such, and therefore all worthwhile things which depend on it, as a mirage, a trap, a futile waste of time.

The upshot of Evagrius's and Thomas's picture of acedia seems to be this: acedia causes us to escape from the sustained effort needed to pursue life's highest ends, and so leads us to betray ourselves. It's a condition of depressed indifference, in which we're drained just by contemplating demanding ends, never mind by the continuous effort they require. Although we might affirm them and need them as buttresses of our identity (as we would put it now), including our social identity, fundamentally we experience them as deadly impositions – destroyers of the pleasures that life could bring – and regard the work they demand as implacably tedious. Taking no joy in them, we lose all love for them and even for life itself. Our existence becomes bearable only by a succession of new stimulae that will excite our nervous system in order to calm it. Slowly our life withers in this desert of ethical neglect.

For the long tradition of acedia, such oppressive sluggishness of the spirit is to be avoided at all costs. For when it is directed at spiritual ends it can bring nothing good, not even the despair that could motivate an overcoming of itself. To be mired in acedia is, ultimately, to be mired in what the great sixteenth-century mystic John of the Cross calls a 'lukewarmness', the very nature of which is 'not to care greatly or to have any inward solicitude for the things of God'.[3] It's a lukewarmness, a not caring, the philosophers of acedia seem to be saying, that ultimately spreads to everything and perhaps everyone, including oneself.

As with regret, however, there is another and very different side to boredom. Far from manifesting only as demoralized sluggishness, it can be the very opposite: a powerful source of new motivation and of fresh perspective on priorities that have become jaded. At least this is how we have come to think about it in the modern age. Fifteen centuries after Evagrius there's been a remarkable revolution in how the boredom of acedia is understood – a revolution that's central to my claim that boredom isn't just enmeshed in a vicious circle with procrastination, as both its cause and its effect, but can also be a key to overcoming it.

Since the early nineteenth century, this revolution in understanding has transformed boredom from being seen only, or principally, as a sin or a disease that alienates us from all that is good, and so foments ruin, to being perceived as a royal route to attaining a more authentic relation to ourselves and the world – and, to that extent, as making possible a free, creative, and flourishing life. Destructive though boredom can be to our projects and well-being, and powerless though it can make us feel, according to this more recent view it can also open up the possibility of a more intimate, more vital, relationship to ourselves and to the world than we habitually seek or sustain. It's a view that has been expressed in a great variety of ways by a litany of writers, from Fernando Pessoa to David Foster Wallace, from Friedrich Nietzsche to Jean-Paul Sartre, and from Aldous Huxley to, above all, Martin Heidegger.[4]

Crucial here is what amounts to a fresh take on Evagrius's observation that the noonday demon of acedia 'makes it appear that the sun moves slowly or not at all, and that the day seems to be fifty hours long'. Evagrius is picturing how profound boredom plunges us into an oppressive awareness of time as it relentlessly fills, surrounds, besieges, and bears down on us in its amorphous longueur. As he vividly describes it, his restless fellow monks crave nothing more than to flee from this oppression to a life free of monotonous discipline. But the boredom-induced awareness of time can also be interpreted in another, potentially life-enhancing, way – namely, as affording an immediate relation with time as the most fundamental reality of living; the reality that discloses us to ourselves and the world to us. As the Nobel Prize-winning writer Joseph Brodsky (1940–96) puts it in his essay 'In Praise of Boredom', boredom 'represents pure, undiluted time in all its repetitive, redundant, monotonous splendor. In a manner of speaking,' he adds, 'boredom is your window on time.'[5]

But the time that the deepest boredom reveals isn't the ticking time of the clock, as when we're stuck in a huge traffic jam or waiting impatiently for a delayed flight. The time that is experienced in such relatively superficial boredom is measurable, linear, and finite; it's a sequence of nows that we know – or expect – will come to an end when the jam eases or the flight's rescheduled time is announced. In deep boredom, time can seem like the world of the fathomless ocean, in which we can find no centre, no periphery, and so no bearings.

Or perhaps even this image of the ocean doesn't get close to the heart of the matter. For if we summon the courage to descend to the depths of boredom – if, as Brodsky urges, we 'go for it', we let ourselves be 'crushed by it; submerge, hit bottom'[6] – we will realize that time isn't merely the medium in which we necessarily exist, as when we say that 'we live in time', or 'the events of my life take place in time'. Rather, in a sense we *are* time.

What I mean here is that our relationship to time, as revealed by boredom, isn't analogous to saying that the ocean is the medium in which the fish necessarily exists. For the fish and the ocean in which it lives – and which is its whole universe – can be understood as distinct from each other. It would make no sense to say that the fish *is* the ocean. By contrast, there's no sense in which I can consider myself apart from time. Thus when I think of what it is for me to be a self, it's obvious that my self isn't just 'in' time – in that it is plonked in an independent flowing thing called 'time', like a swimmer standing in a flowing river or being carried along by a current. Rather, it is comprised of time: of a past – for example as memories and experiences that are active today; of dead loved ones who live on within me – and of a future into which I am constantly projecting, in the form of my priorities, hopes, fears, and so on – a projecting that, like my memories, is not distinct from my self but is constitutive of it. In short, my past and my projected future are always part and parcel of my self as I experience it at any moment. In such a way my self *is* time.

This insight into who we are is given to us with particular intensity by the kind of deep boredom that permits no distraction and therefore no escape. In such boredom we experience the immensity of time – time's unstructured, unticking void – and our sheer nakedness in relation to it. Deep boredom isn't provoked by doing nothing, or by having nothing to do; for *that* still leaves us with the freedom – the prospect – of escape, and indeed of choice. Rather, it is to be mired in all-enveloping tasks in which we find no meaning, or to be trapped in bondage to people with whom we can find no common language. And, still worse, it is to find no meaning in *anything or anyone*: to be cornered in a meaningless world – one of the signature experiences of modernity and surely one reason why modernity is so profoundly familiar with boredom. As the poet Fernando Pessoa (1888–1935), whose day job was to fill in accounting ledgers at a dull company, puts it:

> Tedium is not a sickness brought on by the boredom of having nothing to do, but the worse sickness of feeling that nothing is worth doing. And thus, the more one has to do the worse the tedium. How often have I looked up from the book in which I'm writing and felt my head quite empty of the whole world. It would be better for me if I were inert, doing nothing, with nothing to do, because that tedium, though real, I could at least enjoy. In my present state there is no respite, no nobility, no comfort in feeling discomfort; there is a terrible dullness in every gesture I make, not a potential weariness in gestures I will never make.[7]

Procrastination is so often accompanied by just this feeling of being trapped, even if the project we are procrastinating over originated in a free and wholehearted decision, as it surely did with many of Evagrius's monks when they first embarked on the monastic life. Indeed, the boredom is especially oppressive if occasioned by a project that we chose out of intense inner conviction; for if we cannot find stable meaning here, in what we experience as an authentic choice, then the nightmare prospect opens that we will find stable meaning in nothing. If we feel trapped, even where we take ourselves to have freely chosen, powerless despite our power of self-determination, we will begin to get a sense for the deeper horrors of boredom.

This, however, is exactly where its saving power lies. As with regret, the pain of deep boredom – taking root inside us, 'quiet as the spider . . . spinning its web in the shadowy places of [the] heart', as Gustave Flaubert tells us it did in the heart of Madame Bovary[8] – compels us to ask if the way we are living our lives and if the priorities we've chosen are right for us – no matter how convinced we've been about them. Alongside regret, boredom is the other active agent in procrastination that enables us to reassess our values and ends, shining a searchlight on which of them to abandon for the sake of new ones and which to continue pursuing. Like regret, it can therefore be a powerful impulse to creativity – compelling us to act. Kierkegaard, although no friend of boredom, which, as a Christian philosopher, he held to be 'a root of all evil',[9] wrote that boredom had even induced the God of Genesis to create the world. Seeing the first person he made, Adam, himself become bored, God further created Eve – and from this original couple spiralled out the whole of humankind. Boredom, Kierkegaard says, can be traced back to 'the very beginning of the world': 'The gods were bored so they created man. Adam was bored because he was alone, so Eve was created. From that time boredom entered the world and grew in exact proportion to the growth of population.'[10]

But boredom can bore deeper into our soul than does even regret, causing us not just to abandon old priorities or allow new ones to emerge, but to forge a more intimate, unmediated relation to ourselves and to the world. It can force us into an often frightening, although potentially exhilarating, experience of our raw reality, facing us with our own unprotected presence. A presence expressed not by our values, hopes, and strivings, or by our achievements and productivity, but by our nameless, inarticulate, stubborn, living hereness. Then, if we succumb to it and let it speak to our depths, rather than running away from it, boredom reveals the bedrock of our being: the irreducible existence that isn't dependent on, or defined by, our successes, failures, self-esteem, and status in the eyes of others.

This experience of the raw reality and bedrock of our being is hard to evoke, let alone briefly. It's akin to the 'feeling of existing' ('le sentiment de l'existence') that Jean-Jacques Rousseau describes, alone on the Île Saint-Pierre, a tiny and hard-to-access island in the middle of Lake Bienne in Switzerland, where he lived for six weeks in the summer of 1765. Here he experienced 'a sufficient, complete and perfect happiness which leaves no emptiness to be filled in the soul'. In this bliss, time is an endless present; one deeply enjoys 'one's own existence', and in this sense 'we are self-sufficient like God'.[11] And the very opposite of this self-revelation happens when we do all we can to ignore the reality of boredom – to soldier our way through it or to fidget and deny our way out of it. Nietzsche again puts it beautifully: 'He who completely entrenches himself against boredom also entrenches himself against himself: he will never get to drink the most potent refreshing draught from the deepest well of his own being'.[12]

When we're living life in a managerial, controlling way, and even more so when we're distracting ourselves, we seldom have such unmediated access to our irreducible, vital existence – in all its undeniable yet unpindownable reality.

To gain that access, even if fleetingly, is the greatest gift of boredom – and therefore one of procrastination's greatest blessings. It's a gift that is ours only if we don't flee boredom the moment it unpleasantly touches us, but rather allow ourselves to be immersed in it until we are able to hear what it is telling us – even silently screaming at us – about who we are and who we're not, about misplaced priorities or lifeless ways of going about the right ones. It's a gift that is always hard-earned because tolerating boredom – letting it reveal and guide us to the self that we might have long avoided or blithely passed by like an uninteresting stranger – demands patience of such brutal stubbornness. (Which is perhaps why Nietzsche adds that 'Against boredom even gods struggle'.[13])

Few have evoked the thrill of this gift more vividly than David Foster Wallace (1962–2008) in a note he left with his unfinished novel *The Pale King* – unfinished because while immersed in writing it he committed suicide, at the age of forty-six, following years of the depression that had dogged him since his student days. The note was found by his widow, the artist Karen Green, buried within a pile of hard drives, floppy disks, ring binders, handwritten notebooks, and other motley files. Together they contained the twelve chapters he'd completed in the one-windowed garage where he worked – all of them lying under the glare of lamps that he'd left on before hanging himself:

> It turns out that bliss – a second-by-second joy + gratitude at the gift of being alive, conscious – lies on the other side of crushing, crushing boredom. Pay close attention to the most tedious thing you can find (tax returns, televised golf), and, in waves, a boredom like

you've never known will wash over you and just about kill you. Ride these out, and it's like stepping from black and white into color. Like water after days in the desert. Constant bliss in every atom.[14]

9
Resist the Mirage of Complete Fulfilment

In his late work, *A Confession*, the great Russian writer Leo Tolstoy says this:

> My question, the one that brought me to the point of suicide when I was fifty years old, was a most simple one that lies in the soul of every person, from a silly child to a wise old man. It is the question without which life is impossible, as I had learnt from experience. It is this: what will come of what I do today or tomorrow? What will come of my entire life? Expressed another way, the question can be put like this: why do I live? Why do I wish for anything, or do anything?[1]

Tolstoy was no paragon of humility. Internationally famous in his lifetime, he considered himself 'a celebrity' and had, according to one of his biographers, A. N. Wilson, 'decided implicitly that he was in fact the greatest literary genius in the world'.[2] And yet, approaching fifty, with *War and Peace*, *Anna Karenina*, and numerous other now canonical works behind him, he would agonize about what would come of his life. To the point where the very question – which he saw as latent in every one of us in virtue of our being mortal – led him to contemplate suicide.

For procrastination, it's *the* potentially fatal question: what will come of what I do today or tomorrow? Or: why do I wish for anything, or to do anything? It's not only that we can't possibly foresee the entire chain of consequences of what we do now, let alone of our entire life. It's also that merely to ask this kind of question, especially in the sceptical spirit of a Tolstoy, can destabilize and condemn every priority we cherish – distancing us from it and contaminating motivation with paralysing doubt. The result can be complete resignation, which is exactly, Tolstoy says, what happened to him:

> My life came to a standstill. I could breathe, eat, drink and sleep and I could not help breathing, eating, drinking and sleeping; but there was no life in me because I had no desires whose gratification I would have deemed it reasonable to fulfil. If I wanted something I knew in advance that whether or not I satisfied my desire nothing would come of it.[3]

As a result, the value of even the greatest imaginable worldly success was placed under the gallows of an unanswerable question mark: 'Well, fine, so you will be more famous than Gogol, Pushkin, Shakespeare, Molière, more famous than all the writers in the world, and so what?'[4]

The reality, he concluded, was that 'life is meaningless'. Not long after writing this, his translator Jane Kentish remarks, he would go on, in the early 1880s, to repudiate 'the vanities of literary success, referring to *Anna Karenina* as "an abomination that no longer exists for me"'.[5]

Once it has gripped us, it's very difficult, perhaps impossible, to unask a question like Tolstoy's that can swallow our motivation whole and frame our entire life as pointless. But as one of the most powerful causes of procrastination it's vital that we find freedom from such a question, even if we cannot escape it completely. This, however, is no easy task; in fact, of all my seven proposals for overcoming procrastination, it's by far the hardest to follow. At least that is what I have found.

A very different way of expressing despair about the point of wishing for or doing anything was made by that arch pessimist, the nineteenth-century philosopher Arthur Schopenhauer. Schopenhauer insists that no stable, let alone final, satisfaction is ever available. This, he argues, is grounded in the very nature of desire. If a desire is satisfied you will have only brief pleasure, which will quickly give way to boredom and so either the search for a new desire or else the despair of having none. But if your desire is stymied or yet to be attained you will suffer from frustration. In other words, the satisfaction and thwarting of desire are soulmates, bonded by hopelessness. Either way, we'll suffer – swinging, as Schopenhauer puts it, 'like a pendulum to and fro between pain and boredom', which are 'the ultimate constituents' of our human existence. Striving is an 'unquenchable thirst' and the struggle to find lasting pleasure in the achievement of any of our individual desires and aims is therefore doomed.[6] As he explains:

> All *willing* springs from lack, from deficiency, and thus from suffering. Fulfilment brings this to an end; yet for one wish that is fulfilled there remain at least ten that are denied. Further, desiring lasts a long time, demands and requests go on to infinity; fulfilment is short and meted out sparingly. But even the final satisfaction itself is only apparent . . . No attained object

of willing can give a satisfaction that lasts and no longer declines; but it is always like the alms thrown to a beggar, which reprieves him today so that his misery may be prolonged till tomorrow . . . Thus the subject of willing is constantly lying on the revolving wheel of Ixion, is always drawing water in the sieve of the Danaids, and is the eternally thirsting Tantalus.[7]

To be affixed forever to a revolving wheel, without hope of reprieve, was the torture meted out by Zeus, king of the Greek gods, to Ixion, a ruler of legend, as his punishment for attempting to seduce Zeus's wife, Hera. To pursue desires, Schopenhauer holds, is to be tied to such an interminable wheel of suffering. This is why he sees the highest goal of life as ceasing to desire. Salvation from Ixion's wheel is to liberate the will from all striving for satisfaction.

But success can also be unfulfilling for exactly the opposite reason to Schopenhauer's: not the intolerable boredom of an achieved aim, but the unbearable joy. We're not talking here of joy being unbearable because it becomes addictive as every surge of gratification – every dopamine spike – precipitates craving for a still greater surge just to achieve the same degree of pleasure. Nor are we talking of someone like the triumphant lottery winner, who can finally realize lifelong material dreams but who falls into despair as they turn out to be hollow. Or the retiree, relieved of a life of toil and now in control of their time, plunged into self-destructive depression as their new-found freedom strands them without direction or purpose. We're not even talking about the famous elusiveness of happiness – the impossibility of chasing after it directly; the reality that it is a by-product of leading a life structured by worthwhile ends. Rather, we're talking of someone who cannot tolerate the joy of success itself – who dreads precisely the unmixed happiness of achieving their most valued priorities, and perhaps especially those that are also the most demanding.

In an essay from 1916, Sigmund Freud claims that people can even be 'wrecked by success'. They can 'fall ill precisely when a deeply rooted and long-cherished wish has come to fulfilment. It seems then', Freud continues, 'as though they were not able to tolerate their happiness; for there can be no question that there is a causal connection between their success and their falling ill'.[8]

His explanation for this phenomenon is that conscience, and therefore potential guilt, are what stand in the way. Commenting on this passage, Adam Phillips suggests that, for Freud,

> it is one thing to want something in fantasy, but for it to be gratified in reality is dangerous: it may be a forbidden wish, or an overwhelming pleasure, or a pleasure that creates a dependence; or it may be an enviable pleasure and invite attack. Our pleasures and satisfactions might be at the cost of other people's deprivation and suffering. There are, that is to say, lots of good and interesting reasons, and lots of good and interesting reasons flagged up by psychoanalysis, why pleasure is a problem . . .[9]

Of all the reasons why pleasure can be a problem, the most puzzling are not, however, a feeling of guilt, forbidden wishes, fear of causing harm to others, and concern about arousing their jealousy – or otherwise because conscience obstructs enjoyment. The most puzzling is that joy – especially in achievement or good fortune that powerfully recognizes and affirms who we are, and that bonds us blissfully to our fellow human beings – can be so intense that it endangers our identity and sense of safety. To successfully finish a treasured project; to unexpectedly receive a major prize; to win sudden fame; to feel passionate love for someone who, against all our expectations, requites it with equal force; to finally attain social reform for which one has fought, almost in vain, for years – such deep triumphs can send our mind and heart spinning into confusion. Uncontainable delights threaten to explode us like blasts of air furiously pumped into a balloon: our frame, our being, cannot contain the happiness that fills it. We feel unbearably real to ourselves – and unbearably real in relation to the world – and so we flounder, unsure of what to do with who we've become. Success has bolstered and sharpened our sense of self, which challenges the comfortable vagueness of who we thought we were and maroons us on the island of our own existence. As a result, success – the sense of triumph – can be what we most want and at the same time what we most dread.

That there are degrees of bliss which the human frame cannot accommodate is attested to by the French writer Stendhal (1783–1842) in recollecting a visit he made to Florence in 1817. Beauty, Stendhal wrote in his treatise *On Love*, is 'nothing but the promise of happiness'. But the beauty that he encountered on glimpsing the frescoes of the Baroque painter Baldassarre Franceschini, otherwise known as 'Il Volterrano', in Florence's basilica of Santa Croce must have evoked a vista of happiness so overwhelming that, as he reports in his memoir of the trip:

As I emerged from the porch of Santa Croce, I was seized with a fierce palpitation of the heart (that same symptom which, in Berlin, is referred to as an *attack of nerves*); the well-spring of life was dried up within me, and I walked in constant fear of falling to the ground.[10]

Stendhal's reaction to awe-inspiring beauty became so notorious that it eventually gave rise to a medical term, 'Stendhal syndrome', coined in 1989 by an Italian psychiatrist, Graziella Magherini, the symptoms of which are 'dizzy spells, palpitations, hallucinations, disorientation, loss of identity, and physical exhaustion'.[11]

Nor is Stendhal the only author to give voice to the potentially unendurable power of a promise of happiness. The German-speaking Bohemian poet Rainer Maria Rilke expresses a similar thought in his *Duino Elegies*, a masterpiece composed over the course of a decade after 1912:

> Beauty is nothing
> but the beginning of terror, which we still are just
>   able to endure,
> and we are so awed because it serenely disdains to
>   annihilate us.
> Every angel is terrifying.[12]

But the terrifying power of joy is perhaps most dramatically conveyed by ancient myths where mortals are threatened with death if they should even momentarily look directly at a divine being. Thus, in the Hebrew Bible, when Moses asks God, 'Please show me your glory', God replies with a severe warning: '[Y]ou cannot see my face, for no one shall see me and live.' To be sure that Moses will not accidentally see him, God says: 'While my glory passes by [you, Moses] I will put you in a cleft of a rock, and I will cover you with my hand until I have passed by; then I will take away my hand, and you shall see my back, but my face shall not be seen.'[13] To attain the highest conceivable end for a human being – finding oneself face to face with God – would be annihilating.

What are we to do when a question like Tolstoy's gatecrashes our consciousness with its terrible 'what will come of my entire life?', or 'what will it have all been for?', triggering a crisis of procrastination? When it so plagues us with doubts that none of our priorities, however greatly we cherish them and however successful we've been at pursuing them, has the power to resist it. With the result that they come to lose their grip on us – and even weighty accomplishments come to feel weightless.

When I've been beset by such questions, as I often have, I've found that four kinds of response can help dethrone their power.

The first is that it's impossible to figure out all that will come of my life. And so there's no point asking Tolstoy's question in the first place. It's not only that I can't know the innumerable ramifications of everything I've done. It's also that I can't possibly sum the net value – to myself and to others – of the achievements, meanings, delights, fulfilled desires, and other outcomes I've secured on just *one* of my top priorities, say being a parent or a charity worker or an engineer. Let alone across all of my top priorities. For a start there's no scale on which the varied outcomes of any one of those priorities could be measured – never mind a single scale on which they could all be measured and then aggregated. The purpose and pleasure that I and others derive from, for example, my being a good engineer *and* a good parent *and* a good charity worker in my spare time, are distinct and cannot be summated, or weighed against each other, even if they could be individually known and calibrated. If I were religious I could leave the summation of the value to be found in my life up to an omniscient God; I myself, however, can only keep striving to be the best engineer or parent or charity worker, as I understand those vocations at any given time in my life.

Even on my deathbed, therefore, I won't be able to say exactly what has come of my entire life. And if I can't figure out what will come of my entire life, I will also never be in a position to determine whether I have lived it and fulfilled my potential to the full. *If,* that is, there is such a thing as a maximum potential that we each have, that could be gauged, and that we could ever know we'd reached – all assumptions that I doubt. What's much more likely – as well as much more thrilling and motivating – is that life has no finish line. There is no point at which we *could* be finally and completely fulfilled.

So if I'm one of those people who expects definite answers to questions about what all the things I have pursued and achieved amount to – and how far they've taken me to attaining my full potential – I will need to accept that no such answers are available. It would be absurd – and tragic – for my motivation to be eviscerated when none come.

My second response to Tolstoy's question is that the satisfaction we find in our achievements can be (and I think often, even usually, is) short-lived. That he ceased to be fulfilled by his immense literary triumphs is, in a sense, not strange. But it need not be a reason to lose all faith and delight in our goals themselves. For the reality seems to be that pleasure – and to a lesser extent pain – are hard to remember vividly. Unless they are extreme, taking the form of relived ecstasy or trauma, the particular sensations they unleash usually evaporate from our awareness like smoke in the night. We might retain a strong memory *that* we had pleasure or pain. But eventually no more than a faint trace remains of *how* it felt, which can be recalled only by reliving in our minds, as vividly as we can, the events that occasioned it. (The sense that, for me, seems to recall its own experiences most precisely and reliably, without needing to be presented with them again, is hearing, followed by sight, then smell and taste, and finally touch – the last being the most underrated of the senses, perhaps on account of its poor memory. For example, I can often remember a sustained melody after hearing it once or twice, but I find it hard to summon in my mind the precise taste or smell of, say, a carrot even after eating one countless times. All in all, however, memory can be remarkably ineffective at retaining the rich experience of pleasure.)

Working for years on a demanding project, like a novel, we will derive tremendous joy, as well as a fair measure of torture, from the process of writing it, including from the exercise of such talents and skills as we have. Completing it brings its own special delight. And we further enjoy whatever success it confers. But it's a pipe dream to expect all these sources of satisfaction to *endure*, to remain fresh, and to cumulatively add up to a stable sense of fulfilment robust enough to be always available to us, many years down the track. It's a pipe dream that sets me up for disappointment, which in turn becomes another cause of demotivation and so of procrastination.

That fulfilment can be unstable – that it somehow drains away and must be ever renewed – should not be demoralizing. On the contrary, its fragility is precisely what powers much of our drive to seek new achievements and fresh experiences – the womb of so much of life's richness.

The third answer to Tolstoy – an answer that he himself pursued – is to spend less time concerned with what will come of my life and more devoted to a cause beyond myself. Or differently put: it is to transcend concern for my own flourishing through wholehearted concern for the well-being of others. Such devotion could be to the flourishing of one's family, one's communities, strangers in need, endangered species, the biosphere, even humankind. It would restore to one's life purpose, serenity, and joy in belonging – which the egotistical pursuit of ends that are oriented largely or exclusively to one's own fulfilment is conspicuously unreliable at attaining.

But does even such self-transcendence necessarily answer a crisis of the kind we are speaking of here?

The experience of the great nineteenth-century social reformer and philosopher of liberty, John Stuart Mill, suggests that the answer is no. As philosopher Kieran Setiya, to whose book *Midlife* I owe this example, points out, Mill, like Tolstoy, was a superachiever who fell into catastrophic despair.[14] Where Tolstoy's crisis took him to the verge of suicide, Mill was led to a nervous collapse by the reality that even his noblest ambitions to make the world a better place had mysteriously lost their power to give him joy. Instead, everything that would ordinarily have afforded 'pleasurable excitement' had become 'insipid or indifferent'.

This, at any rate, was the answer to the Tolstoyan question with which, he tells us in his autobiography, he confronted himself:

> Suppose that all your objects in life were realized; that all the changes in institutions and opinions which you are looking forward to, could be completely effected at this very instant: would this be a great joy and happiness to you? And an irrepressible self-consciousness distinctly answered, No! At this my heart sank within me: the whole foundation on which my life was constructed fell down. All my happiness was to have been found in the continual pursuit of this end. The end had ceased to charm, and how could there ever again be any interest in the means? I seemed to have nothing left to live for.[15]

Mill was only twenty when he wrote this, which we might think is far too early for such a characteristically midlife crisis. But he had already tasted huge achievement that might more usually lead to the same crisis of meaning in someone substantially less accomplished and twice his age. Under the private tutelage of his fiercely ambitious father, he had embarked on ancient Greek aged three; Latin at eight, by which time he had also read 'a number of Greek prose authors', including the whole of Herodotus, much of Xenophon, as well as no fewer than the first six books of Plato; Newton's *Principia* at eleven; Aristotle's logic at twelve; and by fifteen he had devoted himself to extensive studies of history, law, political economy, and philosophy, among other disciplines.

It would hardly be surprising if Mill's breakdown was

entirely due to his appallingly intense and lonely upbringing. But his own account suggests otherwise. Amid all this learning he discovered, also at fifteen, that his life purpose was, above all, in action: in social reform. 'I had what might truly be called an object in life; to be a reformer of the world.'[16] He had cared hugely about this; yet now, five years later, at twenty, asking himself how he would feel even if he attained every reform to improve the lives of others that he could imagine, his answer was that such a triumph would leave him empty, without happiness or joy.

We cannot know if Mill's pursuit of social reform was ultimately motivated by the search for his own fulfilment, so that he never achieved self-transcendence. Nor can we know if he was – fruitlessly – expecting dedication to improving the lives of others to provide him with a degree of stable gratification or self-realization that would suffice to, so to speak, 'justify' his life as optimally lived. If such was Mill's motivation and expectation, and if as a result of their frustration he fell into Tolstoy's despair about the point of wishing for anything, it would point to a fourth answer to Tolstoy's question. An answer that might be the key to exiting his labyrinth of despair.

This fourth answer goes roughly as follows. Although, as we said just now, there is no stable state of fulfilment available to us that will give our life a meaning that's immune to doubt, what matters most is the *journey*. Which is what Shakespeare's Cressida surely expresses when she says, 'Things won are done; joy's soul lies in the doing'; what 'Roads are made for journeys, not destinations', a remark sometimes attributed to Confucius, suggests; and what is echoed in a common German saying, 'Der Weg ist das Ziel', 'the path is the goal'. A full and well-lived life, even if it's not the best we could imagine, is one where we richly employ our energies and talents in the *activity* of pursuing those ends we most cherish. A life where fulfilment comes ever anew at each stage of the journey.

And we can go further, as, among many others, Goethe (1749–1832) does: not only is the journey – the doing – at the heart of the meaning to be found in our strivings; at the heart of the journey lies the present moment. It should command our passionate attention. 'Only the present is our happiness', says Faust, the eponymous hero of Goethe's renowned tragic poem, which stretches to over twelve thousand lines. 'Existence is a duty.'[17]

As the philosopher Pierre Hadot (1922–2010) remarks in his illuminating commentary on this scene, Faust needs instruction in how to attend to the splendour of the now. This he receives from Helen of Troy, the most beautiful woman in the world according to Greek legend, with whom he has fallen deeply in love. Sitting, in Goethe's evocation of her, on a throne, next to Faust, he proclaims to her:

> Has the Source of Beauty, overflowing its banks,
> Flowed into the deepest recesses of my being?
> . . .
> To you I dedicate the stirring of all strength,
> The essence too of passion;
> To you, affection, love, worship and madness.[18]

Hadot remarks that the 'art of concentrating on and recognizing the value of the present instant' has been largely lost by modernity, which is dominated by anxious focus on future and past – a focus that, according to the wisdom of the ancients, is deeply misguided. As he reminds us, according to an Epicurean saying: 'The life of a foolish man is fearful and unpleasant; it is swept totally away into the future'.[19] By contrast, the Greeks understand what Goethe called 'the healthiness of the moment'.[20] They understand, as Hadot paraphrases Goethe, how to *be in* the present, to *act in* the present, to *act upon* the present, and to *profit from* the present. In teaching this classical wisdom to Faust, Hadot continues, Helen reveals to him the splendour of the instant and 'teaches him to say yes to [it], to the world, and to himself'.[21]

Goethe is reputed to have proclaimed that, for his own life too, 'The present is the only goddess I adore.'[22] But there is a very important caveat to be made to all this talk about focus on the present, being in the moment, and the value of the journey: it would be a major error to imagine that to be in the now, and in the journey, you must cease being deeply absorbed by goals, let alone empty your mind of all fixation on goals. On the contrary, true focus on the present is best informed and energized by our deepest priorities.

One might riposte that, for example, Zen meditation has no goal. But it does have a goal; indeed, one that demands supreme practice and effort over a lifetime. It is 'the art of seeing into the nature of one's own being, and it points the way from bondage to freedom'. It is 'a discipline aiming at the reconstruction of character', as the famous scholar of Buddhism D. T. Suzuki characterized the Rinzai tradition of Zen.[23] Hardly an activity that can be said to be goalless.

So, too, Schopenhauer's solution to the inevitable suffering caused, he maintains, by all desire, whether satisfied or unsatisfied, is the very real goal of liberating the will from any and all objects of desire. In this self-renunciation of the will he saw salvation. To achieve it, the will that expresses itself in each of us – what he calls the 'will to life' – must turn against and deny itself. Crucially, this isn't a once and for all event. Rather, it must be continually maintained: 'those who have once attained to denial of the will [must] *strive with all their might* to keep to this path by self-imposed renunciations of every kind'.[24] Calming the will takes persistent 'struggle' against our natural tendency to exercise willing, which is 'constantly springing up afresh'. In other words, not only does willing not to will have a goal; not only does it, paradoxically, take sustained striving and struggle; it has an open-ended goal, one that, in Schopenhauer's view, gives life its highest purpose and yet one that no human being could perfectly attain.

A life truly without goals, entirely devoted to the moment, would, I suspect, quickly land us in despair – assuming it were available, which I don't think it is. We can't find all our meaning in contemplating sunsets, going for walks, or mindfulness. And even those activities are often motivated by ends: finding inner peace; meditating on the best way out of a problem we face; deciding on our future priorities; attending to what we value the better to pursue it (a point I will take up in the next chapter). All of us need purpose. We need it to inform the journey and the present. To motivate our attention to them – to what is before us now.

Indeed, there's an intimate two-way relationship between the journey and the goal towards which it's headed.

On the one hand, it is the goal that gives our delight in the journey and our focus on the present much of their meaning and intensity. If I'm building a wooden cabinet or learning a new piece of music, or working to becoming a better carpenter or musician, the richness of the journey or of the present moment is inseparable from the goal that inspires and motivates it. Strikingly, when Faust says that 'only the present is our happiness', he *doesn't* mean this as a devotee of goalless mindfulness. On the contrary, he very much has a goal in mind – and not a modest goal either, but one of the most demanding imaginable. For he is motivated by nothing less than a 'quest for the highest existence'.[25]

Conversely, and at the same time, it's only through immersion in the journey that we deepen our grasp of the goal that inspires and structures it. It's only through striving that the end comes to be more richly defined and intimately present to us. Few ends, including projects such as constructing the cabinet, learning the new piece of music, or writing this book, can be precisely conceived or imagined in advance. Their detailed shape, their point of attainment (if they have one), and their meaning to us evolve – they come to life – with our pursuit of them. So if we labour for years at a project or at a vocation and find that we're still far from knowing precisely where we're going, we should realize that this isn't cause for demoralization – and so for procrastination; rather, it's the natural order of things.

Like Faust, his creation, it's unlikely that Goethe himself ever meant his adoration of the present to exclude or invalidate deep absorption in goals and projects. Indeed, it's impossible: few people in history have been more richly endowed with goals – both lifelong goals and specific projects that those goals ordain – than this poet, playwright, scientist, memoirist, and novelist of genius, who never ceased to strive for the most demanding and long-term ends with staggering consistency of purpose. This is, after all, the poet who, in the most intense devotion to a single project imaginable, devoted a full fifty-seven years, almost his entire literary life, to writing *Faust*. His example confirms that only the trajectory established by ends can give the present moment a poignant joy that would induce us to say to this moment what Faust, before he encountered Helen, couldn't yet say: 'Stop, you are so beautiful!'[26] And calling to mind the two-way relationship between ends and the moment, to which I just alluded, this is a joy that, in turn, intensifies our delight in, and clarifies our understanding of, those very ends.

Which brings us full circle back to Tolstoy's question – the question that propelled him to the verge of suicide: what will come of my entire life?

Our final answer to Tolstoy is that this is the wrong question to ask. For we discover our true fulfilment not through seeking an unavailable answer to what our aims and achievements will finally amount to. Not by attempting to somehow calculate the net value, satisfactions, and disappointments they have so far secured, whether to us or to others. Nor by preserving in the porous aspic of our memory the pleasures we have found in them. Rather, fulfilment lies in immersing ourselves in the splendours of the present that our pursuit of our ends opens up. It is this promise of fulfilment that gives us a reason to wish for things and to persist with them – and ultimately a reason not to procrastinate.

But how do we attain such immersive concentration on the present? And on those ends that imbue the present with power to be our supreme happiness? This brings us to the seventh key to overcoming procrastination that I propose here: cultivating the art of open-hearted attentiveness. It is to this final priority that we now turn.

10

Cultivate Attentiveness

No genuine relationship to the living reality of anything or anyone is possible without attentiveness. We can't immerse ourselves in the present moment – or for that matter in a future informed by our priorities – just by staring at it, or craving it, let alone by our attention darting all over the place. There's no point being in a concert, or spending an evening with your partner, or playing the saxophone if your mind is skidding all over a thousand extraneous preoccupations. Such experience is only twilight experience. To be real we need to be in it with all our being. We need to let its presence impinge on us.

If there's a single precondition for overcoming procrastination, this is it. It is the key to turning our experience of work from a cold, process-driven productivity cult to which we've enslaved our life – and where even brief bursts of attention can be achieved only by constantly cajoling ourselves to concentrate on the task in hand, reinforced by rewards for success and penalties for failure – into one where we feel fully and vitally absorbed in the reality of what we are working on. This state of absorption – of losing ourselves in an activity – is akin to what the psychologist Mihaly Csikszentmihalyi (1934–2021) calls 'flow'.[1] It's an immersed attentiveness to a goal that we deeply care about and it's the key to engaging not just in work but in any activity – from listening to a friend to reading a book to watching a sunset.

Attentiveness is about more than 'focus', which expresses only part of it: the part that travels, like a light, from us to the object, whether it assumes a narrow-angle focus on a specific feature – a single melody – or a wide-angle view – a whole song. It's the part that illuminates the object, turns us towards it, and holds it in view. The other half of attentiveness is about receptivity. Its direction of travel is from the object to us. It strives for a disciplined passivity that lets the object speak; that opens ourselves to it as widely, as patiently, and as sensitively as possible – not just listening to it but hearing it, not just seeing it but noticing it. It's therefore a kind of humility; the real humility, which isn't self-abasement but the power to let ourselves be touched by the reality of what isn't us, so that it may reveal to us who, or what, or how it is. (Not that we'll be able to notice everything about the object of our attention, be it a loved one or a treasured priority. It would be absurd to think that attentiveness can be omniscient. We are necessarily prisoners of partial perspectives and values.)

True attentiveness therefore combines focus and receptivity – holding the object of our attention and letting it hold us. This active passivity, as we might call it, is key to achieving our priorities – and to genuinely relating to anything we value. In love it's the precondition for turning desire for a loved one into an embodied relationship with them; into becoming an enchanted 'we' in addition to being a mutually attracted 'I' and a 'you'. Without it there can be no true dialogue and discovery of who the other is. No devotion that's really about them – their feelings, self-understandings, commitments, needs, and hopes – rather than just about who we think they are and what we need from them. Crucial here is patience – as in Gabriel García Márquez's extraordinary novel *Love in the Time of Cholera*, where Florentino Ariza waits fifty-one years, nine months, and four days for Fermina Daza to reciprocate; a wait that's fruitless, for she never yields to him. Few of us can be that patient; nonetheless, the moral is that to be attentive to a loved one is necessarily to wait with resolute openness for them to turn towards you and perhaps to reveal moments of themselves.

Taken to the level of genius, attentiveness to the real presence of those people and priorities and things we most care about allows every sign of them to flood us with the force of revelation. This, I imagine, is the power of receptivity that enabled Vincent van Gogh, according to a letter he wrote to his brother, to see nineteen distinct shades of white.[2] Or that enables a top chef to distinguish between the taste of a superb apple at its ideal ripeness and just short of it.

But like all talent, even the greatest inborn capacity for attentiveness needs long cultivation. Without it, focus and receptivity will always be fleeting. The psychologist and philosopher William James (1842–1910) put it succinctly: 'there is no such thing as voluntary attention sustained for more than a few seconds at a time'.[3] Both its active and passive aspects need to be schooled like a skill – focus and receptivity equally. For this we have the word of sages, from the Buddha to the Roman Stoics and beyond. Which is why all such traditions prescribe spiritual exercises for training attention to the moment we're actually in. According to the first-century Roman statesman and philosopher, Seneca, in order to learn attentiveness:

One must circumscribe two things: the fear of the future and the memory of past difficulties: the latter no longer concerns me, while the former does not concern me yet ... The sage enjoys the present without depending on the future. Freed from the heavy cares that torture the soul, he hopes for nothing, desires nothing, and does not launch himself into what is doubtful, for he is content with what he has [that is, with the present, the only thing that, according to Seneca, belongs to us]. Do not believe that he is content with little, for what he has [now] is everything.[4]

If we are to attend to the present, Seneca says, we need to practise treating it as our complete happiness. To which we might object that we couldn't possibly be happy in a brutal dictator's prison camp. We would not only hate the present but would dread the future for the further deprivation and torture it might bring. But Seneca would disagree. Even in the helplessness and perhaps hopelessness of the prison, it's in our power to find joy in the now. Indeed, such a moment of joy, he and other Stoics argue, is equivalent to an eternity of joy. Pierre Hadot, the philosopher whom we met in the previous chapter, sums up this Stoic attitude of attentiveness to the present as follows:

For the Stoics, we have everything in the present. The present alone is our happiness, for two reasons: First, because ... Stoic happiness is complete at each instant and does not increase with duration. Next, because in the present instant we possess the whole of reality, and an infinite duration could not give us more than what we possess in the present moment.[5]

Thus, for the Stoics, true attentiveness to the present isn't just one facet of a well-lived life; it's an entire way of life because, in their vision, by being alive to the moment we achieve intimacy with the universe and with eternity. In being attuned to the reality of the moment, we're in harmony with all of reality. Which is happiness. As Seneca puts it: 'He who has lived his entire life every day possesses peace of mind.'[6]

This is not the eccentric teaching of one person, or even one school of thought, but an insight that has found systematic and subtle expression in very different traditions, notably Buddhism. Redolent of Seneca, the 'four noble truths' set out in the historical Buddha's first public teaching at Sarnath in north-east India – subsequently known as *The Discourse on Turning the Wheel of Dharma* – ultimately aim at detaching us from all craving and the inevitable suffering that, the Buddha holds, it brings in its train. As the scholar of Tibetan Buddhism Jay Garfield explains, far from being merely one teaching of Buddhism, the four noble truths are at the very heart of its ethical worldview.[7] They proclaim, first, that all of existence is permeated by suffering (*dukkha*) – a reality that we usually evade, except when we can no longer avoid it. Second, suffering isn't just inflicted on us by causes beyond our control, but is principally rooted in our attachments and aversions – what he calls 'the two faces of craving' – which in turn arise from deep confusion about the nature of reality. This leads to the third truth, which is the need to eliminate these causes of suffering by eliminating the misplaced craving which is at their root. And this, according to Garfield, is about how we *see* the world – our stance towards it – rather than (as many Western approaches to the ethics of overcoming suffering insist) how we *act* in it.

For how we act, according to Buddhist ethical practice, is secondary to how we see.[8]

So what stance are we to cultivate towards the world? The fourth truth addresses this question. At its heart is the 'eightfold path', which Garfield summarizes as 'correct view, correct intention, correct speech, correct conduct, correct livelihood, correct effort, correct mindfulness, and correct meditation'. These don't comprise a sequence of eight steps, each one preparatory to the next. Rather, they're eight dimensions of right conduct which, taken together, constitute a way of life – a way of being.[9]

Attentiveness of a remarkably rich and complex kind is at the very core of the eightfold path. It was pithily characterized by one of the most influential of all Buddhist philosophers, Buddhaghosa, who lived in Sri Lanka around the fifth century CE, as 'the centering of consciousness evenly and correctly on a single object'.[10] Which sounds clear enough, but, as the scholar of Hinduism and Buddhism Jonardon Ganeri emphasizes, there are many distinct aspects to Buddhaghosa's understanding of attentiveness. Take looking at a single leaf. There is the experience of 'producing in mind' (*manasikāra*) that leaf, in other words, the focal attention that centres our mind on the leaf, allowing it to take form in consciousness. Then there's the experience of 'placing thought' (*ekaggatā*) on the leaf, so that we become absorbed by it – and resistant to distractions, such as noticing other leaves. To both these aspects of attention must be added the gathering, through an effort of intention, of all our mental resources (*cetanā*) into, so to speak, the attentive stance. And, critically, all three aspects of attention have to be sustained if we're to persist with even this one task of focusing on a leaf. Which, in turn, means that we need to mindfully rehearse or retain (*sati*) the leaf in our mind – literally bearing it in mind so as to prevent it from 'bobbing out of view'.[11] One of Buddhaghosa's commentators, called Dhammapāla, who also lived around the fifth century, explains that what is meant by this is 'the steadying of an object, remembering and not forgetting it, keeping it as immovable as a stone instead of letting it go bobbing about like a pumpkin in water'.[12]

We don't need to accept all these tenets of Buddhaghosa and Seneca to sense their profound understanding of what it takes to achieve concentrated attentiveness to what lies right before us, in its real presence. We don't, for example, need to accept their claims that suffering is the fundamental existential problem for human beings, which renders life – with its attachments, aversions, and desires – entirely unsatisfactory; and that the elimination of suffering is therefore the supreme end of a well-lived life. Nor do we need to endorse Seneca's mystical belief that the whole cosmos is in the present moment. Nor, above all, do we need to avoid craving a future. In particular, while heeding Seneca's warning that fear of the future and anxious memories of the past destroy attentiveness to the present, we should nonetheless insist on the vital importance of our priorities and projects in informing, energizing, and giving meaning to the present. For such present meaning is key to overcoming the deadening tedium of the now that lies at the very heart of procrastination, and so, in turn, to rekindling motivation in self-sabotaged priorities.

But if we're to be inspired by the power of the present, it's essential to follow the teaching of Buddhism and Stoicism that true attentiveness to it cannot be summoned at a stroke whenever we need to 'concentrate', but rather involves an array of distinct cognitive skills which must all come together to achieve even a moment of full involvement in the world. And that these skills, such as Buddhaghosa's focal attention, placed attention, mindful attention, and attentional effort, each require training over many years.

It's all too easy to imagine that the difficulty of pursuing our priorities and projects resides principally in the actual performing of them, for example, in the technical skill of flying an aircraft, cooking a meal, or performing a surgical operation; of being a considerate spouse or hearing out our children. But attentiveness – as the precondition for pursuing all these activities – can be the most exacting part. The often painful effort of achieving and then sustaining it is perhaps the most potent of all our reasons to procrastinate. And it's a reason to procrastinate that's potentially always there, whereas many of the others come into view sporadically or at particular times of our life – be they fear of mortality, feeling overawed by the stakes of our priorities, or the paralysing 'so what?' that beset Tolstoy.

Given the demands of such effort, it's hardly surprising that, for Buddhism, disengagement 'is the mind's default status' (*bhavaṅga*). Hardly surprising that it sees inattentiveness as 'the state to which it [naturally] returns unless otherwise drawn to engage'.[13]

That Buddhism sees inattentiveness as the mind's natural state has a crucial implication which goes against the overwhelming weight of received opinion today. Distractions are not a principal cause of procrastination. They can exacerbate it, for sure, but the mantra that deems them, and in particular the exploding online universe, the chief culprit in a procrastination epidemic gets things the wrong way around. It sees attentiveness as the mind's default status and imagines that distractions grab us, rather than we them. Misleadingly, distraction has become fetishized as *the* enemy. And we procrastinators are cast as its victims.[14]

Some conditions of inattentiveness will, of course, lie far beyond our immediate control to the extent that they are rooted in powerful genetic, biological, environmental, or social causes. They might manifest as mental illnesses and in the vast, if not uncontroversial, increase since the 1970s in diagnoses of attention deficit hyperactivity disorder (ADHD) in both children and adults – and most recently of a combination of autism and ADHD. For example, one study of children in California reported an increase of 24 per cent in physician-diagnosed ADHD in children aged five to eleven years between 2001 and 2010 alone.[15] And the numbers since then have continued to skyrocket.

Without doubt, distractions lie in wait, like never before, for a mind that's hungry for them or receptive to them, ever more assiduously tracking, beckoning, and manipulating our needs, vulnerabilities, and habits. With our heads firmly stuck in a cloud of bleeps and flashing screens, a barrage of consumer temptations and social media seduces our restless focus to dart in random directions, addicted to the limitless opportunities to search, snoop, cajole, pillory, praise, preen, hate, scream, protest, dox, sleuth, and influence or be influenced.

That the problem is not the actual distraction is attested by Evagrius, the Egyptian desert monk of the fourth century whom we met in our discussion of boredom. The problem is our urge to escape from the difficulty of a demanding life priority. The noonday demon destroys the monk's devotion to God not by seducing him with the bright lights of the city, the beauties of the flesh, the consolations of friends and society, or the alternative life of starting a family. The demon doesn't need all that to do its job. Much more important is the preparatory task: to make the monk fatally irritable, restless, despondent, and disillusioned with the rigours of his vocation; to oppress him with the slow passing of every hour of every day and the daunting prospect of sustaining his devotion to God over an entire lifetime; to induce him to search for that somewhere or someone else, where fulfilment will come more easily. Thus primed, the monk won't need the demon's help to seek out and lunge at distractions from his life's purpose.

Evagrius's near contemporary, Augustine, is also preoccupied with the problem of distraction. Deeply aware of its ubiquity, he laments its temptations in terms that are entirely recognizable to us today:

> When so many things of this kind [a glittering array of pleasurable curiosities and experiences] surround our daily life on every side with a buzz of distraction, when may I be so bold as to say, when can I venture the claim, that nothing of the sort tugs at my attention to go and look at it, and that I am not caught by any vain concern?[16]

And he appeals directly to his own mind to resist the 'buzz' that tugs at his attention to God, the supreme good of his life: 'Do not distract me; that is, do not allow yourself to be distracted by the hubbub of the impressions being made upon you.' Yet Augustine fears that the challenge of resisting the buzz is beyond his powers. And so he turns to God for help in sticking to one of the great tasks he has set for himself (that of investigating the nature of time and existence in God's creation): 'Allow me Lord, to take my investigation further . . . let not my attention be distracted.'[17] For without divine help, he is sure that any passing triviality would capture his attention 'like an empty headed fool' and that his mind is easy prey for random thoughts and desires:

> When I am sitting at home, a lizard catching flies or a spider entrapping them as they rush into its web often fascinates me. The problem is not made any different by the fact that the animals are small . . . My life is full of such lapses, and my one hope is in your great mercy. When my heart becomes the receptacle of distractions of this nature and the container for a mass of empty thoughts, then too my prayers are often interrupted and distracted; and in your sight, while I am directing the voice of my heart to your ears, frivolous thoughts somehow rush in and cut short an aspiration of the deepest importance.[18]

Clearly, anxiety about distraction is far from confined to us moderns. As Evagrius and Augustine attest, it extends back for at least a millennium and a half, just as concern about what we today call procrastination does. Nonetheless we are living at a time of peak concern about the power of distraction to blow our lives off course – and especially about how to find our way out of the online maze once we've been addictively sidetracked into it.

It's certainly true that a welter of evidence points to ever-shortening attention spans, not just since the dawn of the internet age but since at least the late nineteenth century –

when the pace of economic growth, international connectedness, and information flow began to accelerate in earnest.[19] According to one estimate, three minutes is the average length of time that an American office worker stays on one task.[20] Once derailed, they might have to struggle for a full twenty-three minutes to regain the same state of focus.[21] Another study, by the psychologist Gloria Mark, suggests that the average time that people, working on their computers or any other screen, spend on a task before switching to something else has plummeted from two and a half minutes in 2004 to seventy-five seconds in 2012 and, most recently, forty-seven seconds.[22]

Some researchers, such as a group at King's College London's Centre for Attention Studies, question such conclusions on the grounds that there isn't yet enough data to support them. Based on a survey undertaken in September 2021, the King's College team argue that 'the absence of long-term research means it remains unknown whether technology has [really] caused a deterioration in the . . . ability to concentrate' – although the survey showed that people tend to *believe* that it has. In answer to questions such as 'Does our modern information environment worsen our attention spans? Or are we over-estimating the impact of technology on our lives?', the authors conclude that 'comparisons with survey data from previous decades indicate that, on some measures, the public *at least feel* more pressures [to be distracted] than they did in the past'.[23]

But even if the evidence for collapsing attention spans turns out to be conclusive, it doesn't follow that measures to sever us from the temptations of distraction are the go-to solution. Block apps, like Freedom, that prevent access to websites; screen-time controllers such as ScreenZen;

noise-cancelling headphones; a safebox where I can put my devices and be unable to retrieve them for however many hours I've programmed it to lock; digital detoxes – these and other tricks for controlling our online addictions aren't enough. They're not enough even when combined with such well-worn recommendations as establishing three daily priorities, focusing on challenging work rather than tending to emails and social media, and setting deadlines with limited time – say fifty minutes rather than the whole afternoon – such as Chris Bailey advances in the *Harvard Business Review*.[24] Putting distractions beyond our reach might be key in situations of intense vulnerability, such as we face in periods of great stress or deep depression, or when we're edgy, overly vigilant, and depleted of motivation. Or when no attentiveness in the world could resist an overwhelming source of seduction, such as Homer's Odysseus faces on encountering the beautiful sirens who lure sailors to their death with their sweet but deadly song. Knowing that even his legendary resolve couldn't withstand such temptation, he has his crew tie him so tightly to the mast of their ship that he's unable to succumb to their lethal trap. The mythical equivalent of a total internet block.

Ordinarily, however, imposing external restrictions on our access to distractions won't tackle the problem of inattentiveness, and more broadly the challenge of unleashing motivation. For one thing, although they can lock out some external distractions, there are still plenty left which are harder to debar: reordering the desk, flicking through a handy magazine, grazing on food, eavesdropping on a nearby conversation. Not to mention internal avenues of avoidance or displacement, such as daydreaming about an exotic vacation or fantasizing about a romance. Like water, restlessness naturally finds the path of least resistance.

As in the times of Evagrius and Augustine, all those centuries ago, the real problem is quite different. It's our craving to flee goals to which we're devoted – which is precisely the problem that we've been discussing throughout this book. When today we get 'sucked' into the online world, it isn't always the latest ping that's drawing us in, or the thrill of a virtual mob tearing apart an unfortunate victim – in its more extreme manifestations the contemporary equivalent of condemned criminals being eaten alive by lions mad with hunger for the entertainment of a baying audience in the Colosseum of ancient Rome (the so-called *damnatio ad bestias*, or 'condemnation by beasts'). For all the power of social media platforms to capture our attention, and to survey, monetize, and manipulate our behaviour, including our voyeuristic addictions, the longing to get drawn into distractions springs, deep within us, from the urge to avoid the pain of attentiveness – and to seek the pleasure of release from it. We 'let ourselves be tempted', as dieters might say when deciding not to refuse a delicious piece of cake, because we believe or hope that distraction (always experienced as temporary) will relieve the strenuousness of sustained attention to what we really want – but is hard to do. This is why the key to the problem of distraction is not to find ingenious ways to debar ourselves from it, but to train attention as Buddhaghosa and Seneca teach us to do.

Conclusion:
When Procrastination Can Be a Blessing

I've proposed seven ways to overcome procrastination, which, taken together, offer a new approach to tackling the avoidance that's most damaging to our well-being: dodging those select ends that we see as crucial to our flourishing and our identity. Conventional solutions that advise us to formulate our top priorities and focus on more efficient time management won't suffice in such cases – not only because we already have our top priorities but also, and crucially, because our main challenge here isn't time management; it's unleashing our innate motivation to pursue what we most care about – motivation that's already there, deep within us, somehow frozen.

To achieve that unleashing of motivation, I'm recommending a very different approach, the aim of which is to give us a new freedom and focus to pursue our highest life goals by *changing our perspective* on them: how we think about them, how we relate emotionally to them, what we expect from them, how we attend to them.

This change of perspective begins with lowering the stakes of our priorities. Which we might achieve by reimagining them as an escape from what we ought to be doing; by worrying less about the recognition they will or won't secure; by discarding the myth of perfection; by discovering the empowering freedom in visualizing the insignificance of our projects and lives in a vast universe that cares nothing for our existence. The point is to bring us into deeper intimacy with our priorities by making them less paralysingly overwhelming and less subservient to the hoped-for approbation of others, be they contemporaries or posterity.

Having freed our priorities of oppressive stakes, we should pursue them, as far as we can, in a spirit of play. In other words, instead of regarding their pursuit as a productivity-dominated, process-driven Sisyphean treadmill, we should recast it as an experimental, nimble, joyful free play, which is intensely absorbed in the present but still serious and goal-directed – just as the play of children can be.

At the same time, we must find a way of keeping our mortality at the forefront of our minds – and in particular the reality that, as transient creatures, death is an ever-present possibility. Not to panic over limited time, which never sustainably motivates us. Rather, to bring us into a more authentic relationship with our own life – a vibrant closeness to our own self – such as those diagnosed with an incurable disease often find, or as it has been evoked in ancient myths of heroes who descend into the world of the dead in order to return to living with new wisdom, vitality, and clarity of purpose.

Which brings us to two often destructive but also potentially creative emotions occasioned by procrastination: regret over the time stolen by it and the deep boredom in which it can submerge us. The challenge here is this: rather than being demoralized or immobilized by regret and boredom, or attempting to ignore or deny them, we should allow them to do their real job, which is to motivate us to examine whether our priorities are right for us – and, if they are, to rededicate ourselves to them afresh; or, if they're not, to seek different goals. We should harness their formidable power to be a wake-up call that we've chosen a wrong or a stale path; to tell us that our ambitions are unsuited to us, even when they're strongly held. Or that their aims are too ill-defined. Or that how we inhabit them is unthinking and ossified by routine. For regret and boredom often harbour just such a message with unnerving persistence and extraordinary clarity.

Yet, everything we hope for and are motivated to seek can be sabotaged if we're in thrall to the mirage of complete fulfilment; the expectation that there should come a time when we feel stably and finally fulfilled. It's a mirage which feeds on ancient misconceptions, such as that we have a potential capable of being fully defined and attained; or that we could ever know, even on our deathbed, what our life adds up to, whether in terms of happiness or achievements. Instead I've argued that fulfilment lies most reliably in deep absorption in the journey, and even in the present moment. Such absorption must of course be informed by our ends – indeed, it is given much of its intensity and meaning by them – but our focus on our ends and their accomplishment mustn't be exclusive, as it is when it comes at the expense of our love for the present.

Finally, we must cultivate attentiveness: the resolute, patient, unequivocating, ardent focus on and receptivity to the present. This involves a capacity to wait, listen, and look often without knowing what we are waiting, looking, and listening for. And it is key to achieving full involvement in any task – and so to overcoming procrastination.

I'm not suggesting that we can or should follow all seven of these proposals, never mind at once. Two or three that work best for us might suffice. Nor do I underestimate how hard it is to pursue them if we're trapped, without any vision of an exit, by poverty, discrimination, soul-destroying jobs, arduous responsibilities, or unhappy relationships. Changing the spirit in which we live and work might then be impossible. But insofar as we possess the necessary freedom and resources to seek such a many-sided transformation in how we relate to priorities on which we're stuck, the aim of doing so is to re-engage with them with new freshness, so that we can unshackle our underlying motivation to pursue what most matters to us.

At the same time as proposing this new approach to overcoming procrastination, my discussion has also thrown up a caveat, which has threaded its way through the book: *procrastination isn't always an affliction*. Our response to it shouldn't invariably be to find a way to soldier on with our stuck priorities. Sometimes it's sending us a very different message. Its despair – in particular caused by regret and boredom, the subject of the fourth and fifth of my recommendations – might be telling us that we are on the wrong path, adopting life-ends, embarking on projects, and embracing values that aren't suited to who we are. Or that what we must change isn't our priorities but rather the stifling manner in which we're going about them; that we need to seek a new spirit in which to pursue them, a spirit which is freer of precisely the managerial-technocratic ethos of the cults of autonomy and work as they have developed in the West. In other words, procrastination can be a rebellion against stale priorities and soulless routines – a refusal, arising deep within us, to go on as before.

Easily sucked into the eddies of life, as many of us are, we might go through decades without ever pausing to demand of ourselves whether we should change course – especially if we've been successful at it. Conviction that we should is often extinguished by dread of writing off even brief investments of time and effort, never mind years of them. By unclarity about what new directions to pursue along with fear of losing social status by starting afresh. And by the crude rule of habit, which dulls our emotional responses through long repetition and clouds our awareness of whether and how to change[1] – the habit that Marcel Proust describes as a 'heavy curtain [that] conceals from us almost the whole universe, and prevents us from knowing ourselves'.[2]

Sometimes only the stubborn pain of procrastination can break the deadlock. Only its agonizing stuckness has the disruptive power needed to refocus our life on different goals more deeply aligned with who we are – or to recommit us with new zeal to priorities we've been avoiding, or pursuing in lacklustre ways. Then, what we might have seen as a 'sickness' becomes the key to health, echoing T. S. Eliot when he writes: 'Our only health is the disease / . . . / to be restored, our sickness must grow worse.'[3]

The pain can be intense; but it is redeemed in dedicating ourselves anew to cherished priorities or in motivating us to discover others that we're able to genuinely love. A still worse pain is to discover too late, when our brightest energies are gone, that we have spent our best years in tepid pursuit of ends to which we're indifferent – having sensed all the while that we should move on but somehow failing to do so or even to know what we really want. E. M. Forster beautifully evokes that quandary in his novel *A Passage to India*, when an Englishman, prompted by his inability to experience the moment of an exquisite sunset, reflects on his whole life and realizes that he has never inhabited it – that 'he experienced nothing himself'. Over forty years, Forster writes of his character,

> he had learnt to manage his life . . . had developed his personality, explored his limitations, controlled his passions – and he had done it all without becoming either pedantic or worldly. A creditable achievement, but as the moment passed, he felt he ought to have been working at something else the whole time, – he didn't know at what, never would know, never could know, and that was why he felt sad.[4]

Submitting to any potentially transformational pain, along with its biting frustration at wasted life – so that we learn from it – takes great courage. As Adam Phillips remarks, inspired by Freud, letting ourselves feel our frustration 'is a surprisingly difficult thing to do'.[5] If we refuse the feeling we won't achieve 'a sense of what it is we might be wanting, and missing; of what might really give us pleasure'. For in Freud's story, 'it is only in states of frustration that we can begin to imagine – to elaborate, to envision – our desire'. For the founder of psychoanalysis, our capacity for frustration is the source of our possibilities for satisfaction, and specifically of 'the inspiration for our unlived lives'. This is because all development, and most fundamentally the development of selfhood from earliest childhood, depends on 'an awareness of something necessary not being there'.

Often, if not usually we merely *fantasize* jumping the gap between what we are and what we want to be, in Phillips' words, 'as if by magic'. To *actually* jump the gap by switching the course of our lives is quite different. And procrastination, with its intense frustration, can be precisely what motivates us to do so.

A great advance of our time is that it has increasingly given us the freedom to jump the gap; to change our minds and our direction throughout our lives, not only on romantic commitments, marriage, and sexual, gender, and community identity, but also on vocation, on career, and – less often remarked, but vitally – on education. More opportunities exist than perhaps ever before to switch career path as our interests develop and as undiscovered talents manifest themselves, as well as to retrain, upskill, refresh our knowledge, and learn new disciplines – rather than, as was once the case, fixing (or, often, merely falling into) all these choices in our early adult years, or already in adolescence. For all the lingering prejudice against hiring or even taking seriously people in older age groups, there, too, possibilities are mushrooming.

And it isn't just opportunity to switch vocation and lifestyle that's increasingly being extended to people in their thirties, forties, fifties, or later, but also and crucially social approval. Where once abandoning a career path and starting again was denigrated as evidence of a flip-flopping inability to make up one's mind or jack-of-all-trades amateurism, now it's ever more accepted – and even admired for its bravery and openness to new horizons. It is perfectly feasible, as a musician friend of mine showed when she embarked on studies in nursing in her early fifties, or as my mother's surgeon turned potter friend confirmed, to change vocation in one's sixties, and – if blessed with sufficient health and financial security into later decades – to enjoy a thriving new life at a time when people might once have languished

CONCLUSION

rudderless at home in their fraying slippers. What surprised and delighted me in both those cases – the nurse and the potter – is that, after their switch, they weren't beset by humiliation at starting from the beginning, surrounded by peers otherwise in the prime of their lives, and denuded of the status they'd enjoyed in their previous professions. On the contrary, bolstered by admiration they received, they had a spring in their step that they couldn't have acquired in any other way.

Strikingly, both had been propelled by those twin active agents engendered by procrastination: regret and boredom. They had listened to these harshest of teachers, neither becoming demoralized by them nor sticking, in immobilized defiance, to a previous trajectory that could never yield deep satisfaction; nor lunging at any more quickly available life that was preferable to their old one.

Why did it take them so long? Many obvious reasons, among them raising children, earlier opposition from family and friends, fear of forfeiting wider social status, and the risks of dropping a successful career for a venture that might fail. But perhaps also something more than that: timing – life's mysterious sovereign, whose ordinances must be obeyed, and who tells us when we are ready to embark on a treasured end, and when the time is not yet ripe.

I want to conclude with this final lesson that procrastination can teach us: the lesson of when the time for a priority or for change has come. Or hasn't. Not every time in life is the right time – a reality that's easy to ignore when the cult of autonomy tells us that now is as good as ever for the choosing and controlling will; that we should look inside, decide what our true aims are, and just go for it. For it can be perilous to come too early to our vocation or to an important aim, goal, or relationship. Blunders, diversions, wrong turnings, wasted effort, long delays, and passion invested in activities that we're good at but not wholehearted about – all these can turn out to be vital preparation for the main task. So, too, is the right experience, the right courage, and the necessary relaxation of internal resistances such as fear of success, fear of failure, fear of becoming someone different from the person I have always been, or the even more powerful but hard to define fear of becoming real to oneself. Just as it can take a big part of a lifetime until we're ready to receive, be changed by, and act on difficult knowledge – of, say, family traumas or self-destructive patterns of relating – so it can take many years until we're ready to discover our true priorities.

Premature conviction about who we are can be not only impotent but paralysing. As Nietzsche puts it, there are great dangers in our spirit coming 'too soon to "understand itself"', so that it doesn't allow time for what he calls the 'organizing "idea"', that true guide of our life, to take shape within us.[6] For the organizing idea does more than map a future; it does more than articulate an end goal. It's also an active force that commands us, that seeks out the individual skills which will one day be indispensable to achieving its aims, and that marshals them into a coherent fighting force. It needs to do all this – and to *learn* how to do all this – at its own pace, which can be very gradually. And it needs to do so well before it is ready to reveal itself definitively to our consciousness. This is why to attempt to discover and lunge at who one is before all these preparatory developments have been given time to unfold, can prevent one from becoming who one is. For some, this moment of readiness will come when they're young, or even still in childhood. For others, it will let itself be known only at later stages after they've tried, failed, tried again, and, in Samuel Beckett's famous words, managed to 'fail better'.

Procrastination, with its brute relentlessness, can be the only sign that's unmistakable and irresistible enough to get us to heed the message that now is not yet the time – that we need to wait, and meanwhile to listen out for that inner voice, which announces the outcome of what Plato calls the 'silent dialogue of the soul with itself',[7] and which might point us to the path forward. When it will speak to us we cannot know in advance. But our paralysis will compel us to wait until it does.

The wisdom of timing is an ancient one. In the monotheistic traditions it goes back to the book of Ecclesiastes in the Hebrew Bible, which, according to rabbinic tradition, was composed by King Solomon, who built the first temple of Jerusalem and who is revered by all three monotheisms: Judaism, Islam, and Christianity. Ecclesiastes proclaims that '[f]or everything there is a season, and a time for every matter under heaven': a time to 'build up' and a time to 'break down'; and, central to our purposes here, 'a time to seek and a time to lose; a time to keep and a time to throw away; a time to tear and a time to sow'.[8] It is echoed by T. S. Eliot in the magnificent music of the *Four Quartets*, when he writes:

> Houses live and die: there is a time for building
> And a time for living and for generation
> And a time for the wind to break the loosened pane
> And to shake the wainscot where the field-mouse trots
> And to shake the tattered arras woven with a silent motto.[9]

CONCLUSION

Finally, a day comes when procrastination seems to relax its grip on us. Gradually, or swiftly, it melts away, and we find ourselves in a clearing of the dark forest in which it had held us. Here, the right path – our path – comes into view; and, perhaps for the first time, we know how to take it. This is the moment of illumination when clarity of mind, energy of purpose, and the calm of focus break through, and we are set on our way towards a goal we might have long sought. Looking back, the often prolonged period trapped in inertia seems as unfathomable to us as how and why our abrupt release came to pass. What we do know is that we now have a sureness that feels genuine, if only because it feels grounded in that metabolization of experience as a result of which what had once seemed beyond our grasp now lies firmly within our purview and our reach.

In such a moment of transition – for which we must prepare ourselves but which we can never merely summon – not only have we been liberated from procrastination, but procrastination has itself become manifest as a great liberator rather than a maddening jailor. Then, far from being an unalloyed problem, it shows itself to be a blessing that can impose on us the necessary time to allow our ruling priorities to germinate and to develop the skills and experiences that they need if they are to blossom – so enabling them to reach a maturity that cannot be rushed.

Acknowledgements

I was privileged to have, in succession, two superb editors: first Sarah Caro, while she was publishing director at Basic Books UK and, after she left, Nick Davies, managing director of John Murray Press, both part of the Hachette family. I am deeply grateful to Nick and Sarah for their inspiring guidance and challenging proposals, without which this book would be much the poorer. Fulsome thanks, too, to Caroline Westmore for managing the transformation of my typescript into a printed book with a deftly firm hand, to Hilary Hammond for her painstaking copy-editing, to Laurence Cole for proofreading, and to Tim Ryder for creating a fine index. I had the great good fortune to benefit from comments on the text, at various stages, from John Cottingham, Anthony Gottlieb, Andrew Huddleston, and Bernard Reginster, and thank them for their time. As ever, I am indebted to my research assistant, Sarah Pawlett-Jackson, from whose unflagging attention to detail and

ACKNOWLEDGEMENTS

always-fruitful comments I have benefited here, as I have over the years. I owe huge thanks to my wonderful agent Caroline Michel and to all the team at Peters, Fraser and Dunlop literary agency. Finally, I cannot sufficiently acknowledge the support and invaluable suggestions of Tamar Abramov, not least in my moments of despair about my glacial progress – and, yes, my procrastination – in the early stages of writing this book.

Notes

Chapter 1: Putting Off Our Most Cherished Priorities

1. T. S. Eliot, 'Burnt Norton', part III, in *Four Quartets*, Faber & Faber, 1949, p. 10.
2. Romans 7:15. Taken from the *Holy Bible: New Revised Standard Version*, Anglicized Edition, Oxford University Press, 1995. All subsequent citations from the Bible, unless otherwise stated, are from this translation.
3. Augustine, *Confessions*, book VIII, ch. 7 (17); trans. Henry Chadwick, Oxford University Press, 1991, p. 145.
4. Oliver Burkeman, *Four Thousand Weeks: Time Management for Mortals*, Penguin, 2021, p. 236.
5. Cal Newport, *Slow Productivity: The Lost Art of Accomplishment without Burnout*, Penguin, 2024.
6. I owe this latter proposal in particular and much in this paragraph in general to discussion with Bernard Reginster, with gratitude.
7. I owe references to the Egyptian hieroglyph and Hesiod to Maria Konnikova, who in turn cites Piers Steel in 'Getting over Procrastination', *New Yorker*, 22 July 2014.

NOTES

8. Anna Katharina Schaffner, *Exhaustion: A History*, Columbia University Press, 2016, p. 15.
9. This section on the Hindu theory of the humours is indebted to Wendy Doniger, 'Medical and Mythical Constructions of the Body in Sanskrit Texts', in *On Hinduism*, Oxford University Press, 2014, p. 207.
10. This paragraph is indebted to Schaffner, *Exhaustion*, especially pp. 52–4.

Chapter 2: The Cult of Work

1. The *Oxford English Dictionary* locates the first transitive use of 'procrastinate' in 1569 and the first intransitive use in 1548.
2. Juliana Menasce Horowitz and Nikki Graf, 'Most U.S. Teens See Anxiety and Depression as a Major Problem among their Peers', Pew Research Center, 20 February 2019; Rachel Minkin and Juliana Menasce Horowitz, 'Parenting in America Today', Pew Research Center, 24 January 2023.
3. I owe the phrase 'total work' to Josef Pieper, who, in his analysis of the high Middle Ages, intriguingly suggests that work for work's sake is the result of the restlessness that is in turn generated by idleness: Josef Pieper, *Leisure: the Basis of Culture*; trans. Alexander Dru, Fontana Library, 1965, p. 40.
4. This point, and all my remarks about Luther and Calvin here, are indebted to Michael Sandel, 'Great Because Good', in *The Tyranny of Merit: What's Become of the Common Good?*, Allen Lane, 2020, ch. 2.
5. Ibid., pp. 38–40.
6. Jonathan Edwards, 'The Preciousness of Time' (1734), in *Sermons and Discourses 1734–1738*, ed. M. X. Lesser, *The Works of Jonathan Edwards*, vol. 19, Yale University Press, 2001, p. 251.
7. Samuel Johnson, *The Rambler*, no. 134, Saturday, 29 June 1751, in Samuel Johnson, *Selected Essays*, ed. with an introduction and notes by David Womersley, Penguin, 2003, pp. 222–6, at p. 223.

8. Thomas Carlyle, 'Labour', in *Past and Present*, Barnes & Noble, 1843, III, p. 245.

Chapter 3: The Cult of Autonomy

1. Kant went still further, proclaiming that even Jesus must be subject to the same moral law that each of us autonomously wills; otherwise the ends that he ordains will not be genuinely moral: 'Even the Holy One of the Gospel must first be compared with our ideal of moral perfection before he is recognized as one'. Immanuel Kant, *Groundwork of the Metaphysics of Morals*, Ak 4:408; trans. and ed. Mary Gregor and Jens Timmerman, Cambridge University Press, 2011, Second Section, p. 45.
2. J. B. Schneewind, *The Invention of Autonomy*, Cambridge University Press, 1998, pp. 512–13, who glosses the highest good as (to employ Kant's rather technical language) the 'harmonious totality of ends that are governed by the moral law'.
3. Friedrich Nietzsche, *Thus Spoke Zarathustra*, First Part, section 17; trans. and ed. Walter Kaufmann, *The Portable Nietzsche*, Penguin, 1954, p. 175.
4. Amber Payne, 'Rachel Dolezal on Rihanna, Her DNA test, "Fraud" claims and Other Facebook Questions', *NBC News*, 28 March 2017.
5. Friedrich Nietzsche, *The Genealogy of Morals*, 'Preface', section 1; trans. and ed. Walter Kaufmann, Vintage, 1989, p. 15.
6. Friedrich Nietzsche, *The Gay Science*, section 335; trans. and ed. Walter Kaufmann, Vintage, 1974, p. 263.
7. John Maynard Keynes, 'Economic Possibilities for Our Grandchildren' (1930), in *Essays in Persuasion*, W. W. Norton, 1963, pp. 358–73.
8. Michael Young, *The Rise of the Meritocracy*, Routledge, 1958.
9. Sandel, *Tyranny of Merit*, p. 10, citing data from 2017. It is, of course, deeply ironic that many of the multiplying diatribes against the cults of meritocracy – and indeed of work – are

spearheaded by some of their most prominent practitioners and beneficiaries. Sandel's polemic against meritocracy is authored by one of its high priests and, as a senior professor at Harvard, a pillar of perhaps the world's most elite meritocratic nursery. Josh Cohen's screed against excessive work, *Not Working: Why We Have to Stop* (Granta, 2020), hails from the pen of one who is not just the author of eight books but also engaged in no less than two professions, being both a professor of literature and a practising psychoanalyst. The ultimate example, however, of a prolific polymath who professes himself disgusted by the cult of work is Bertrand Russell, one of the most relentless workers of all time – author of dozens of volumes, philosopher, mathematician, political activist, broadcaster, university professor, and Nobel Prize winner – who in *In Praise of Idleness* proclaims 'in all seriousness' that 'the road to happiness and prosperity lies in an organized diminution of work' (Routledge, 1935, p. 3). Perhaps these illustrious polemicists are in pole position to rail against their own ways of living because they know best of what they speak; or perhaps they exemplify the seventeenth century's aphorist La Rochefoucauld's maxim that 'hypocrisy is the homage that vice pays to virtue' – although neither explanation in any way diminishes the persuasiveness of their invective. If so, I plead guilty to the same hypocrisy in writing about procrastination.

10. Sandel, *Tyranny of Merit*, p. 22.
11. 'Iron cage' is the evocative term coined by pioneering sociologist Max Weber (1864–1920).
12. Fred Lewsey, 'Would You Prefer a Four-Day Working Week?', University of Cambridge, 21 February 2023, www.cam.ac.uk/stories/fourdayweek; 'The Results Are In: The UK's Four-Day Week Pilot', Autonomy, February 2023, https://autonomy.work/wp-content/uploads/2023/02/The-results-are-in-The-UKs-four-day-week-pilot.pdf
13. 'The Results Are In', p. 65.
14. Lewsey, 'Would You Prefer'.

Chapter 4: Lower the Stakes

1. Bertrand Russell, *The Conquest of Happiness*, Routledge, 2015, p. 62.
2. Robert Benchley, 'How to Get Things Done: One Week in the Life of a Writing Man', *Chicago Tribune*, 2 February 1930.
3. Rhonda L. Fee and June P. Tangney, 'Procrastination: A Means of Avoiding Shame or Guilt?', *Journal of Social Behavior and Personality*, vol. 15, no. 5, 2000, pp. 167–84, at p. 181. I owe this reference to Chrisoula Andreou and Mark D. White, *The Thief of Time: Philosophical Essays on Procrastination*, Oxford University Press, 2010, p. 92.
4. Marcus Aurelius, *Meditations*, book VII, section 34; trans. Martin Hammond, Penguin Classics, 2014, p. 89.
5. Jean-Jacques Rousseau, 'Discourse on Inequality', in *The Discourses and Other Early Political Writings*; trans. Victor Gourevitch, Cambridge University Press, 2nd edn 2018, p. 187.
6. W. H. Auden, 'In Memory of W. B. Yeats', in *Selected Poems*, ed. Edward Mendelson, Faber & Faber, 1979, pp. 80–3.
7. Marcus Aurelius, *Meditations*, book VII, section 6; trans. Hammond, p. 83.
8. Blaise Pascal, Pensée 102, in *Pensées and Other Writings*; trans. Honor Levi, ed. with introduction and notes by Anthony Levi, Oxford University Press, 1995, no. 102, p. 26.
9. Quoted in Guy Kahane, 'Our Cosmic Insignificance', *Nous*, vol. 48, no. 4, 2014, pp. 745–72, at p. 745. Sagan's quote is taken from *Cosmos*, Random House, 1980, and Hawking's from a 1995 Channel 4 TV show, *Reality on the Rocks: Beyond Our Ken*.
10. Thomas Curran and Andrew P. Hill, 'Perfectionism Is Increasing over Time: A Meta-analysis of Birth Cohort Differences from 1989 to 2016', *Psychological Bulletin of the American Psychological Association*, vol. 145, no. 4, 2019, pp. 410–29. I owe this reference to Sandel, *Tyranny of Merit*, p. 181.
11. Fee and Tangney, 'Procrastination'. However, some psychological studies have suggested that perfectionism rooted in standards

set by oneself does not issue in appreciable procrastination. See, for example, Piers Steel, 'The Nature of Procrastination: A Meta-analytic and Theoretical Review of Quintessential Self-regulatory Failure', *Psychological Bulletin*, vol. 133, no. 1, 2007, pp. 65–94, at p. 76.

12. Curran and Hill, 'Perfectionism Is Increasing', p. 410. Curran and Hill cite the following influential 1990 study: Randy O. Frost et al., 'The Dimensions of Perfectionism', *Cognitive Therapy and Research*, vol. 14, no. 5 (1990), pp. 449–68.
13. Curran and Hill, 'Perfectionism Is Increasing', p. 410. Here the authors refer to P. L. Hewitt and G. L. Flett, 'Perfectionism in the Self and Social Contexts: Conceptualization, Assessment, and Association with Psychopathology', *Journal of Personality and Social Psychology*, vol. 60, no. 3, 1991, pp. 456–70.
14. Aristotle, *Metaphysics*, book V, ch. 16, line 1021b15; W. D. Ross, trans., *The Basic Works of Aristotle*, ed. Richard McKeon, Random House, 1941, p. 1103.
15. Allan Mallinger, 'The Myth of Perfection: Perfectionism in the Obsessive Personality', *American Journal of Psychotherapy*, vol. 63, no. 2, 2009, pp. 103–31, at p. 109.
16. Friedrich Nietzsche, *Beyond Good and Evil*, section 78; trans. with commentary Walter Kaufmann, Vintage, 1966, p. 81.
17. Mallinger, 'Myth of Perfection', p. 110.
18. Quoted in Paul Wijdeveld, *Ludwig Wittgenstein, Architect*, 2nd edn, Pepin Press, 2000, p. 173 (my italics). I owe this citation to Richard Sennett, *The Craftsman*, Penguin, 2009, p. 254, to which this section on Wittgenstein is indebted.
19. Wijdeveld, *Ludwig Wittgenstein, Architect*, p. 173; Sennett, *The Craftsman*, pp. 254–5.
20. Hermine Wittgenstein, 'Familienerinnerungen', quoted in Wijdeveld, *Ludwig Wittgenstein, Architect*, p. 148; Sennett, *The Craftsman*, p. 257.
21. Wijdeveld, *Ludwig Wittgenstein, Architect*, p. 173; Sennett, *The Craftsman*, p. 254.
22. Sennett, *The Craftsman*, pp. 254–5.

NOTES

Chapter 5: Remember We Are Mortal

1. I thank John Richardson for pointing this out to me.
2. Martin Heidegger, *Being and Time*, section 250; trans. John Macquarrie and Edward Robinson, Blackwell, 2007, p. 294.
3. Tim Jonze, 'How Cancer in My 30s Brought Me Face-to-Face with Death', *Guardian*, 8 April 2023.
4. Homer, *The Odyssey*, book X, lines 519–23; trans. Robert Fagles, Penguin, 2006, p. 245. The quotations that follow are, respectively, from book X, lines 533–5, 539–45, 619–22 and 626–7, and book XI, lines 21 and 723–7; trans. Fagles, pp. 245, 248, 250, and 270.
5. For a more extended discussion of Odysseus's confrontation with death, and its role in enabling him to recover his true home, see my *Love: A New Understanding of an Ancient Emotion*, Oxford University Press, 2019, pp. 154 and 157–9. I also draw on these extracts from *The Odyssey* in that discussion.

Chapter 6: Embrace the Spirit of Play

1. References to Nietzsche in this paragraph are, respectively, from *The Gay Science*, section 341, p. 274, and 'Thus Spoke Zarathustra', section 1, in *Ecce Homo*; trans. Walter Kaufmann, Vintage, 1967, p. 295.
2. Sigmund Freud, 'Creative Writers and Day-Dreaming' (1908), in *On Freud's Creative Writers and Day-Dreaming*, ed. Ethel S. Person, Peter Fonagy, and Servulo Augusto Figueira, Routledge, 2018, p. 4.
3. References to Nietzsche in this paragraph are, respectively, from *Beyond Good and Evil*, section 94, p. 83, and *Thus Spoke Zarathustra*, First Part, section 1, 'On the Three Metamorphoses', p. 139.
4. Heraclitus, fragment XCIV (D.52), *The Art and Thought of Heraclitus*; trans. and ed. Charles H. Kahn, Cambridge University Press, 1979, pp. 227–9. These possible meanings of *aiōn* are advanced by Kahn, p. 228.

5. Armand D'Angour, 'Plato and Play: Taking Education Seriously in Ancient Greece', *American Journal of Play*, vol. 5, no. 3, 2013, pp. 293–307, at p. 296. This entire paragraph is deeply indebted to D'Angour.
6. Plato, *Laws*, book VII, at 803d–e (my italics), cited in Johan Huizinga, *Homo ludens: A Study of the Play-Element in Culture*, Routledge, 2014, p. 19.
7. Huizinga, *Homo ludens*, pp. 5, x, and 173 (my italics).
8. Ibid., p. 132.
9. Ibid., p. 18.
10. Steven Johnson, *Wonderland: How Play Made the Modern World*, Penguin, 2016, pp. 3–4.
11. Donald R. Hill, *Medieval Islamic Technology: from Philo to al-Jazari, from Alexandria to Diyār Bakr*, Ashgate, 1998, pp. 231–2, cited in Gunalan Nadarajan, 'Islamic Automation: A Reading of Al-Jazari's *The Book of Knowledge of Ingenious Mechanical Devices* (1206)', in *Media Art Histories*, ed. Oliver Grau, MIT Press, 2007, pp. 163–78, at p. 163.
12. Johnson, *Wonderland*, p. 5
13. Ibid., p. 7.
14. Ibid., pp. 9–10.
15. Ibid., p. 83.

Chapter 7: Harness the Power of Regret

1. Adam Phillips, *Missing Out: In Praise of the Unlived Life*, Penguin, 2012, pp. 117 and xviii–xix.
2. Ibid., p. 140.
3. Aristotle, *Nicomachean Ethics*, book VII, ch. 8, lines 1150b29–31, cited in James Warren, *Regret: A Study in Ancient Moral Psychology*, Oxford University Press, 2022, p. 98.
4. Warren, *Regret*, p. 105 and p. 99 citing Aristotle, *Eudemian Ethics*, book II, ch. 8, lines 1224b19–20 (trans. Brad Inwood and Raphael Woolf, Cambridge University Press, 2012): here Aristotle remarks

that 'the person who lacks self-control [*akratēs*] enjoys obtaining the object of his appetite by his uncontrolled behaviour, but feels anticipatory pain arising from the thought that he is doing something bad'. My discussion of Aristotle and Plato on the relation between regret and *akrasia* is much indebted to Warren.
5. Aristotle, *Nicomachean Ethics*, book VII, ch. 3 passim, especially lines 1147a8–10 and 1147b13–19.
6. Ibid., book VII, ch. 3, lines 1147a18–23.
7. Søren Kierkegaard, *Papers and Journals: A Selection*; trans. and ed. Alastair Hannay, Penguin, 1996, p. 63 (original Danish, n. 2).
8. Ibid., 1843, *Papirer* IV, A, 164, p. 161.
9. Ibid., 2 February 1839, *Papirer* II, A, 347, p. 101.
10. Ibid., p. 64.
11. Clare Carlisle, *Philosopher of the Heart: The Restless Life of Søren Kierkegaard*, Penguin, 2019, p. 21.
12. Ibid., pp. 21–2.
13. Ibid., p. 24
14. Ibid.
15. *Kierkegaard's Journals and Notebooks*, p. 164, JJ, 115, 17 May 1843. I owe this citation to Carlisle, *Philosopher of the Heart*, p. 6.
16. Carlisle, *Philosopher of the Heart*, p. 6.
17. *Søren Kierkegaard's Journals and Papers*, pp. 213–14, *Papirer* III, A, 1, 4 July 1840, quoted in Carlisle, *Philosopher of the Heart*, p. 19. My whole discussion of Kierkegaard and Regine, and the conclusions I draw from it in this paragraph, are deeply indebted to Carlisle's study.

Chapter 8: Let Boredom Save Us

1. Evagrius, *Praktikos* 12, in *Evagrius of Pontus: The Greek Ascetic Corpus*; trans. with introduction and commentary by Robert E. Sinkewicz, Oxford University Press, 2003, p. 99.
2. Thomas Aquinas, *Summa Theologiae*, vol. XXXV, 2a2e, 34–46; trans. Thomas Heath, Cambridge University Press, 2006, question

35, p. 23. All my other quotes from Thomas Aquinas are taken from here.
3. St John of the Cross, *Dark Night of the Soul*, book I, ch. 9, section 3; trans. E. Allison Peers, Burns & Oates, 1976, p. 58.
4. My discussion of boredom here is deeply, and above all, indebted to Heidegger, although it in no way claims to be a faithful exegesis, let alone a critique, of his philosophy of boredom.
5. Joseph Brodsky, 'In Praise of Boredom', in *On Grief and Reason*, Penguin, 1995, pp. 104–13, at p. 109.
6. Ibid., p. 108.
7. Fernando Pessoa, *The Book of Disquiet*, ed. Maria José Costa; trans. Margaret Jull Costa, Profile Books, 2017, p. 375. Entry for 19 September 1933.
8. Gustave Flaubert, *Madame Bovary*, Part One, ch. 7; trans. Geoffrey Wall, Penguin, 1992, p. 34.
9. Søren Kierkegaard, 'Crop Rotation', in *Either/Or: A Fragment of Life*; trans. Alastair Hannay, Penguin, 2004, p. 228.
10. Ibid.
11. Jean-Jacques Rousseau, 'Fifth Walk', in *Reveries of a Solitary Walker*; trans. Peter France, Penguin, 1979, pp. 88–9.
12. Friedrich Nietzsche, *Human, All Too Human: A Book for Free Spirits*, vol. 2, section 200; trans. R. J. Hollingdale, Cambridge University Press, 1986, p. 359.
13. Friedrich Nietzsche, *The Antichrist*, section 48; *Portable Nietzsche*; trans. and ed. Kaufmann, p. 628.
14. David Foster Wallace, *The Pale King*, Penguin, p. 548. My remarks on the scene in Wallace's office, discovered after his suicide, are indebted to the Editor's Note by Michael Pietsch in this same volume.

Chapter 9: Resist the Mirage of Complete Fulfilment

1. Leo Tolstoy, 'A Confession', in *Leo Tolstoy: A Confession and Other Religious Writings*; trans. Jane Kentish, Penguin, 1987, pp. 34–5.

I was reminded about this work of Tolstoy and directed to most of the passages from it cited in this chapter by Kieran Setiya's *Midlife: A Philosophical Guide*, Princeton University Press, 2017, p. 38.
2. Tolstoy, 'Confession', p. 31; A. N. Wilson, *Tolstoy*, Atlantic Books, 2015, p. 489.
3. Tolstoy, 'Confession', p. 30.
4. Ibid., p. 29.
5. Jane Kentish in the translator's introduction to *Leo Tolstoy: A Confession and Other Religious Writings*, p. 7.
6. Arthur Schopenhauer, *The World as Will and Representation*, vol. I; trans. E. F. J. Payne, Dover Publications, 1966, p. 312.
7. Ibid., vol. I, p. 196.
8. Sigmund Freud, 'Some Character-types Met within Psychoanalytic Work' (1916), cited in Adam Phillips, *On Giving Up*, Penguin, 2024, p. 59.
9. Ibid., p. 60. My discussion of the fear of success is indebted to Phillips.
10. Stendhal, *Rome, Naples and Florence*; trans. Richard N. Coe, Calder Publications, 2010, p. 302.
11. G. Magherini, *La Sindrome di Stendhal*, Ponte Alle Grazie, 1989, cited in Iain Bamforth, 'Stendhal's Syndrome', *British Journal of General Practice*, vol. 60, no. 581, 2010, pp. 945–6.
12. Rainer Maria Rilke, *Duino Elegies*; trans. and ed. Stephen Mitchell, Vintage, 2009, I, pp. 2–3.
13. Exodus 33:18–23.
14. Setiya, *Midlife*, ch. 2.
15. John Stuart Mill, *Autobiography*, Penguin, 1989, p. 112. This section on Mill draws on and is deeply indebted to Setiya's discussion of Mill in *Midlife*.
16. Mill, *Autobiography*, p. 111.
17. Goethe, *Faust Part II*, act III, lines 9381–2, cited in Pierre Hadot, *Philosophy as a Way of Life*, ed. Arnold I. Davidson, Blackwell Publishing, 1995, p. 222. My discussion of Goethe here, and all references to his *Faust*, are deeply indebted to Hadot.

18. Goethe, *Faust Part II*, act I, lines 6487–500; Hadot, *Philosophy as a Way of Life*, p. 217.
19. Seneca, *Letters to Lucilius*, letter 15, section 9; trans. Hadot in *Philosophy as a Way of Life*, p. 223. My comment on the Stoics here is indebted to Hadot's discussion.
20. Hadot, *Philosophy as a Way of Life*, p. 220.
21. Ibid., p. 221.
22. Goethe, *Goethes Gespräche*, vol. I, 232 (interview with Friederike Brun, Karlsbad, 9 July 1795), cited in Pierre Hadot, *Don't Forget to Live: Goethe and the Tradition of Spiritual Exercises*, University of Chicago Press, 2023, p. 1.
23. D. T. Suzuki, *Essays in Zen Buddhism*, Souvenir Press, 2011, pp. 25 and 27. Though often criticized as adjusted to Western taste and Western conceptions of religious experience, Suzuki's interpretations of Zen remain highly influential.
24. The quotations from Arthur Schopenhauer in this paragraph are from *The World as Will and Representation*, vol. I, pp. 391–2, cf. p. 412 (my italics). This paragraph is indebted to Christopher Janaway, *Schopenhauer*, Oxford University Press, 1994, p. 115.
25. Goethe, *Faust Part II*, act I, line 4685; Hadot, *Philosophy as a Way of Life*, p. 217.
26. Goethe, *Faust Part II*, act V, lines 11580–6; Hadot, *Philosophy as a Way of Life*, p. 124.

Chapter 10: Cultivate Attentiveness

1. Mihaly Csikszentmihalyi, *Flow: The Psychology of Optimal Experience*, Harper & Row, 2008.
2. Vincent van Gogh, quoted in Alasdair MacIntyre, *Edith Stein*, Continuum, 2007, p. 20.
3. William James, *The Principles of Psychology*, Perlego, 2018, ch. 11, p. 404.
4. Seneca, *Letters to Lucilius*, letter 78, section 14; trans. Hadot in *Don't Forget to Live*, p. 22.

NOTES

5. Hadot, *Don't Forget to Live*, p. 22.
6. Seneca, *Letters to Lucilius*, 101.10; trans. Hadot in *Don't Forget to Live*, p. 23.
7. Jay L. Garfield, *Buddhist Ethics: A Philosophical Exploration*, Oxford University Press, 2022, pp. 5 and 71.
8. This paragraph, and in particular the summary of the 'four noble truths', is indebted to Garfield, especially ibid., pp. 4–11, cf. pp. 71–89.
9. All quotes in this paragraph are from Garfield, ibid., pp. 11–12, and my remarks are, again, indebted to him.
10. Buddhaghosa, *The Path of Purification* (*c.* 450 CE), cited in Jonardon Ganeri, *Attention, Not Self*, Oxford University Press, 2017, p. ix.
11. Ganeri, *Attention, Not Self*, p. 66.
12. Dhammapāla, Pm. 487; cited in Ganeri, *Attention, Not Self*, p. 233. Dhammapāla is commenting on Buddhaghosa, whose thought is at the heart of Ganeri's study and therefore of my remarks here.
13. Ganeri, *Attention, Not Self*, p. 68.
14. This is the tenor of, for example, Johann Hari's book, *Stolen Focus: Why You Can't Pay Attention*, Bloomsbury, 2022, as evidenced by its very title.
15. D. Getahun *et al.*, 'Recent Trends in Childhood Attention-Deficit/Hyperactivity Disorder', *Journal of the American Medical Association (Pediatrics)*, vol. 167, no. 3 (2013), pp. 282–8.
16. Augustine, *Confessions*, book X, ch. 34 (56); trans. Chadwick, p. 212.
17. Augustine, *Confessions*, book XI, ch. 27 (36), and book XI, ch. 18 (23); trans. Chadwick, p. 233.
18. Augustine, *Confessions*, book X, ch. 35 (57); trans. Chadwick, p. 213.
19. Interesting research to back up this claim is summarized in Hari, *Stolen Focus*, pp. 27–30 and 272–5.
20. Research of Professor Gloria Mark, cited ibid., p. 8.
21. Study of Professor Michael Posner, cited ibid., p. 10.
22. Gloria Mark, *Attention Span: Finding Focus for a Fulfilling Life*, HarperCollins, 2023, pp. 18 and 95.
23. The Policy Institute, 'Do We Have Your Attention? How People

Focus and Live in the Modern Information Environment', February 2022, https://www.kcl.ac.uk/policy-institute/assets/how-people-focus-and-live-in-the-modern-information-environment.pdf (my italics).
24. Chris Bailey, 'Four Strategies for Overcoming Distraction', *Harvard Business Review*, 30 August 2018.

Conclusion: When Procrastination Can Be a Blessing

1. For a superb account of habituation see Tali Sharot and Cass R. Sunstein, *Look Again: The Power of Noticing What Was Always There*, Little, Brown, 2024.
2. Marcel Proust, *The Captive/The Fugitive, In Search of Lost Time*; trans. C. K. Scott Moncrieff and Terence Kilmartin, rev. D. J. Enright, Vintage, 1996, vol. V, p. 621. I owe this quote to Clare Carlisle, *On Habit*, Routledge, 2014, p. 2.
3. T. S. Eliot, 'East Coker', part IV, in *Four Quartets*, pp. 20–1.
4. E. M. Foster, *A Passage to India*, Penguin, 2021, p. 199.
5. Phillips, *Missing Out*, pp. xix–xx, from which all quotes in this paragraph and the next are drawn.
6. Nietzsche, 'Why I Am So Clever', in *Ecce Homo*; trans. Kaufmann, section 9. Nietzsche variously expresses this thought about an 'organizing idea', around which one's whole life will take shape, in terms of (a) dominating 'drives', (b) a 'personal providence', and (c) a 'single taste'. These citations are, respectively, from *Beyond Good and Evil*, section 6; *The Gay Science*, section 277; and *The Gay Science*, section 290.
7. Plato, *Sophist*, at 263e3–263e5; trans. Nicholas P. White, Hackett, 1993.
8. Ecclesiastes 3:1–7 passim.
9. T. S. Eliot, 'East Coker', part I, in *Four Quartets*, p. 15.

Index

Index

acedia
   Evagrius of Pontus on,
      121–2, 125–6
   as flight from joy, 122–4
   John of the Cross on, 124–5
   Thomas Aquinas on, 122,
      123–4
   see also boredom; distraction;
      'noonday demon'
ADHD (attention deficit
   hyperactivity disorder), 17,
   163
Aeneas, 83
Aeneid (Virgil), 83
afterlife, 16, 74
Ainslie, George, 18
aiōn, 93
akrasia, 107, 108, 109, 110,
   120–1
al-Jazari, Ismail, 97

Anna Karenina (Leo Tolstoy),
   136
Aristotle
   on *akrasia*, 107, 108, 109–10
   on knowledge, 108–9
   on perfection, 66, 70
   on procrastination, 15
   on regret, 107, 109, 110, 192
      n. 4
astrology, 17
attention deficit hyperactivity
   disorder (ADHD), 17, 163
attention spans, 165–6
attentiveness
   Buddhaghosa on, 160–1, 162
   Buddhism and, 157, 161–2
   cultivation of, 157
   difficulty of achieving, 162,
      168
   focus *v.* receptivity, 156

INDEX

attentiveness (*cont.*)
  patience and, 157
  as precondition for love, 156–7
  to present moment, 152, 155–6, 157–9, 161–2, 173
  recent decline in, 165–6
  Seneca on, 157–8
  Stoicism and, 157, 161–2
  William James on, 157
  see also distraction; inattentiveness; patience
Auden, W. H., 59
Augustine (theologian), 9–10, 164–5
authenticity, 76, 114–15, 115, 125
autism, 163
autonomy, 33–6, 38, 40, 43–4, 55–7
  age not yet permitted as subject of, 35
  authenticity and cult of, 76
  constraints on, 37–8
  expanding imperium of cult of, 34–5
  Immanuel Kant on, 33–4, 187 n. 1
  managerial-technocratic ethos of cult of, 174
  moral perspectives on, 33–4, 38, 187 n. 1
  need for recognition and cult of, 57
  opposition to cult of, 40
  procrastination caused by cult of, 36–8
  regret and cult of, 103–4
  spirit of play compared with cult of, 96
  timing in life and cult of, 178
  see also meritocracy

Babbage, Charles, 98
Bailey, Chris, 167
Banū Mūsà bin Shākir, 96–7
Basilica di Santa Croce, 140–1
beauty, 35, 140–1
Beckett, Samuel, 180
Benchley, Robert, 50
bhavaòga, 162
Bible, Hebrew, 141–2, 180
bliss, 130, 131–2, 140
  see also boredom; happiness; joy; pleasure
Book of Ingenious Devices (*Kitāb al-hiyal*; Banū Mūsà bin Shākir), 97
Book of Knowledge of Ingenious Mechanical Devices (*Kitāb fī ma 'rifat al-hiyal al-handasiyya*; Ismail al-Jazari), 97
boredom, 115–16, 119–20
  and authenticity, 125
  as conduit to bliss, 131–2
  David Foster Wallace on, 131–2
  deep, 126, 127–9, 129
  Evagrius of Pontus and, 126
  Fernando Pessoa on, 128

INDEX

Friedrich Nietzsche on, 130, 131
  as impulse to creativity, 129
  Joseph Brodsky on, 126
  and life priorities, 129, 131, 172–3, 174, 178
  as result of procrastination, 129, 131
  as result of satisfaction of desire, 137
  role in origin of humanity, 129
  as route to self-revelation, 129–30, 130–1
  Søren Kierkegaard on origin of, 129
  as source of motivation, 125
  and time, 126–7
  see also acedia; bliss
Brodsky, Joseph, 126
Buddha, 157, 159
Buddhaghosa, 160–1, 162
Buddhism, 157, 159–61, 161–2, 162
  Zen, 149
Burchell, Brendan, 42
Burkeman, Oliver, 10, 74
business innovation, 98

Calvin, John, 25, 26
  see also Reformation, Protestant
Camus, Albert, 62
career
  as displacement activity, 8–9
  increasing opportunities to change, 177–8
  see also work
Carlisle, Clare, 112–13, 114
Carlyle, Thomas, 28
causes of procrastination, 12–13, 162
  anxiety regarding value of accomplishments, 136–7, 142
  contemplation of unlived life, 104
  cult of autonomy, 36
  cult of work, 21–2, 29–30
  desire for posthumous recognition, 58
  difficulty of achieving attentiveness, 162
  failure to accept short-lived nature of fulfilment, 144–5
  fear of death, 76–8
  fear of failing to achieve life priorities, 105–6
  fear of failing to secure esteem, 53
  fear of self-reality, 140
  fear of success, 137–9, 140
  indecisiveness, 27
  lack of attentiveness, 31, 162
  meritocracy, 40
  paralysing significance of life priorities, 49
  perfectionism, 63, 64, 65, 66, 68, 189 n. 11
  premature sense of self-awareness, 179–80
  regret over choice of life priorities, 104
  tepid acceptance of mortality, 77

INDEX

Centre for Attention Studies, King's College London, 166
cetanā, 160
Charaka Samhita (medical text), 16
children, 92–4, 163
  see also teenagers
Cohen, Josh, 188 n. 9
Cohen, Leonard, 58
colleges, 64
  see also universities
computer programming, origin, 98
Condorcet, Marie-Jean-Antoine-Nicolas de Caritat, Marquis de, 66
Confession, A (Leo Tolstoy), 135
Confessions (Augustine), 9–10, 164–5
conscience, 139
cosmos, *see* universe (cosmos)
craving, 159, 161
  see also desire
Csikszentmihalyi, Mihaly, 155
Curran, Thomas, 64, 67

'Dance Me to the End of Love' (Leonard Cohen), 58
D'Angour, Armand, 94
Dante, 83
deadlines, 53, 167
death, 13, 58
  direct confrontation with, 83
  ever-present possibility of, 74, 75, 76, 78, 83–4, 172

fear of death as cause for procrastination, 76–8
  joy in face of, 79
  motivating perspectives on, 75
  solitary nature of, 75, 76
  see also mortality
depression, 68, 167
Descartes, René, 33
desire, 137–8, 149–50
  see also craving
Dhammapāla, 161
Discourse on Turning the Wheel of Dharma, The, 159
displacement activities, 7–9, 12, 13, 50, 51–3, 167–8
distraction
  Augustine on, 164–5
  declining attention spans and, 165–6
  digital, 162, 163, 165, 166–7, 168; *see also* social media
  Evagrius of Pontus on, 121–2, 163–4
  not principal cause of procrastination, 162–3
  from pursuit of life priorities, 163, 164–5, 168
  from pursuit of vocation, 121, 122, 164
  restlessness as precondition for, 121, 122, 164
  restricting exposure to sources of, 166–8, 168
  see also acedia; attentiveness; inattentiveness; restlessness
Divine Comedy (Dante), 83
dolce far niente, 7

Dolezal, Rachel, 35–6
drink-driving, 108–9
Duino Elegies (Rainer Maria Rilke), 141
dukkha, 159
Durkheim, Émile, 28

Ecclesiastes, 180
education, 177
Edwards, Jonathan, 26–7
'eightfold path', 160
ekaggatā, 160
Eliot, T. S., 6, 175, 180
employee welfare, 42
Enlightenment, 66
esteem, 53–4, 55, 56, 57, 62
   see also recognition
ethnicity, 35–6
Evagrius of Pontus, 120, 163–4
   on *acedia* and 'noonday demon', 121–2, 125–6
existence
   as creation of God, 123
   Jean-Jacques Rousseau on sentiment of, 57, 130
   Johann Wolfgang von Goethe on, 148, 151
   reclamation of own, 61

fame, transience of, 60–1
Faust (Johann Wolfgang von Goethe), 148, 149, 151, 152
fear, 13
   of death, 76–8
   of failing to achieve life priorities, 105–6
   of failing to secure esteem, 53
   of self-reality, 140
   of success, 137–9, 140
Fee, Rhonda, 53
Flaubert, Gustave, 129
focus, 156, 157
   see also attentiveness
Forster, E. M., 175–6
'four noble truths' (Buddhism), 159–60
Four Quartets (T. S. Eliot), 180
Four Thousand Weeks: Time Management for Mortals (Oliver Burkeman), 10
Franceschini, Baldassarre ('Il Volterrano'), 140
Freud, Sigmund, 92–3, 139, 176
frustration, transformational potential of, 105, 176–7
fulfilment
   achieved through journey towards life priorities, 147–8, 149, 150–2, 152, 173
   Arthur Schopenhauer on, 137–8
   and desire, 137
   and happiness, 139, 140
   Johann Wolfgang von Goethe on, 148
   John Stuart Mill on, 146, 147
   Leo Tolstoy and lack of, 143–4
   mirage of complete, 173
   of potential in life, 143

INDEX

fulfilment (*cont.*)
   self-transcendence as route to, 145
   short-lived nature of, 143, 144–5
   Sigmund Freud on, 139

Galen, 17
Ganeri, Jonardon, 160
García Márquez, Gabriel, 157
Garfield, Jay, 159–60
gender, 35
goals, *see* life priorities (goals)
God, 26, 121, 143, 164–5
   creation of world arising out of boredom of, 129
   destruction by looking directly at, 141–2
   devotion to, 25, 120, 122–3
   rejection of, 15, 16, 61
   superseding of authority of, 34
Goethe, Johann Wolfgang von, 148, 149, 151
Great Resignation, 41
Groundhog Day (Harold Ramis film), 88–90, 90, 91
guilt, 139

habit, 175
Hadot, Pierre, 148–9, 158
Hannay, David, 111–12
happiness, 138–9, 140, 141, 148, 158, 159
   see also bliss; joy; pleasure
'happiness economics', 41
Hawking, Stephen, 62
Hebrew Bible, 141–2, 180

Heidegger, Martin, 75–6, 78, 125
Heraclitus, 93
Hesiod, 14
Hill, Andrew P., 64, 67
Hill, Donald, 97
Hippocrates, 16
Homer, 80
Homo ludens (Johan Huizinga), 94–6
Homo sapiens, 95
Huizinga, Johan, 94–6
humanity
   divine boredom and creation of, 129
   indifference of universe to, 61–2
   as playful species, 94–6
'humours', 16–17
Huxley, Aldous, 125

idleness (indolence), 6, 26, 186 n. 3
immortality, 58–9
   see also recognition: posthumous
impatience, 15
   see also patience
'In Memory of W. B. Yeats' (W. H. Auden), 59
'In Praise of Boredom' (Joseph Brodsky), 126
In Praise of Idleness (Bertrand Russell), 188 n. 9
inattentiveness
   ADHD and, 163
   Buddhism on, 162

as natural state, 162–3
see also attentiveness;
distraction
indecisiveness, 27
indolence (idleness), 6, 26, 186
n. 3
innovation, 96–8
internet, 162, 165, 166, 168
see also social media
Ixion, wheel of, 138

James, William, 157
Jazari, Ismail al-, 97
Jesus, 187 n. 1
John of the Cross, 124–5
Johnson, Samuel, 27–8, 28
Johnson, Steven, 96, 98
Jonze, Tim, 78–9, 83
journey, the, 147, 148, 149,
150–2, 152
see also present moment, the
joy
acedia as flight from, 122–4
in face of death, 79
in one's own existence, 130
playful experimentation and,
87, 96
in present moment, 152,
158
unbearableness of, 138–42
see also bliss; happiness;
pleasure

Kant, Immanuel, 33–4, 187 n. 1
katabasis, 83
see also death
Kentish, Jane, 136

Keynes, John Maynard, 37
Kierkegaard, Søren
as amorous procrastinator,
110–14
on boredom, 129
on existential choices, 115
regret impelling authenticity
in, 114–15
Kitāb al-ḥiyal (Book of Ingenious Devices; Banū Mūsà bin Shākir), 97
Kitāb fī ma 'rifat al-ḥiyal al-handasiyya (Book of Knowledge of Ingenious Mechanical Devices; Ismail al-Jazari), 97
knowledge, effective *v.* rote,
108–9, 109

La Rochefoucauld, François de,
188 n. 9
laziness, *see* indolence (idleness)
legacy, 58–61
life priorities (goals), 13, 36–7
anxiety caused by importance
of, 49
attentiveness as key to
pursuing, 162
and boredom, 129, 131,
172–3, 174, 178
cost of perfectionism
regarding, 67
discovery of true, 179, 181
distraction from pursuit of,
163, 164–5, 168
fear of failing to achieve,
105–6

life priorities (goals) (*cont.*)
   fulfilment achieved through journey towards, 147–8, 149, 150–2, 152, 173
   impact of need for esteem on choice of, 57
   influence of unconscious on, 110
   lowering stakes of, 49–53, 62–3, 171–2
   in pre-modern times, 103
   and present moment, 161
   procrastination as stimulus to re-evaluate, 175
   raising stakes of, 73
   recast as displacement activities, 50, 51–3
   and regret, 103–4, 106, 107, 109, 110, 115, 172–3, 174, 178
   unknowability of value of accomplishing, 142–3
   see also vocation
love, 123–4, 156–7
Love in the Time of Cholera (Gabriel García Márquez), 157
Luther, Martin, 26, 33
   and origin of cult of work, 25
   see also Reformation, Protestant

Madame Bovary (Gustave Flaubert), 129
Magherini, Graziella, 141
Mallinger, Allan, 67, 68
managerial-technocratic ethos, 42–3, 44, 174
   see also productivity
managerialism, 24, 28–9
manasikāra, 160
Marcus Aurelius, 55, 60
Mark, Gloria, 166
marriage, 24, 112, 114, 115
   see also romantic relationships
memory, 144
   see also recognition: posthumous
mental illness, 163
   depression, 68, 167
meritocracy, 38–40, 67
   expression at point where cults of autonomy and work interact, 38
   opposition to, 43–4, 187 n. 9
Merlin, John-Joseph, 98
metameleia, 107
Midlife: A Philosophical Guide (Kieran Sétiya), 145
Mill, John Stuart, 145–7
mindfulness, 150
modernity, 16, 33, 128, 148
monks, 25, 120–2, 126, 128
   see also Evagrius of Pontus
moral perspectives
   on autonomy, 33–4, 38, 187 n. 1
   on cult of work, 25, 28, 38
   on procrastination, 15, 22
mortality, 16, 73–80, 172
   and choice, 77–8
   Martin Heidegger on, 75–6, 78

INDEX

procrastination caused by
    tepid acceptance of, 77
  as source of motivation, 73–6,
    77, 78, 79–80, 83–4
  see also death
Moses, 141–2
mythology, 80–3, 138, 141
  see also Odysseus

'nepo' classes, 39, 56
neuroscience, 18
Newport, Cal, 11
Nietzsche, Friedrich, 62, 125
  on boredom, 130, 131
  on despising oneself, 68
  as intellectual descendant of
    Immanuel Kant, 34
  life-affirmation test, 90–1
  'organizing idea', 179, 198 n. 6
  on play, 93
  on self-knowledge, 37
  on timing in life, 179
  on truth, 35
'noonday demon', 121–2, 125–6, 163–4
  see also acedia
Not Working: Why We Have to Stop (Josh Cohen), 188 n. 9

Odysseus, 80–3, 83, 167
Odyssey (Homer), 80–3
Olsen, Regine, 111–14
On Love (Stendhal), 140
'organizing idea' (Friedrich Nietzsche), 179, 198 n. 6
  see also timing in life

pain, memory of, 144
Pale King, The (David Foster Wallace), 131–2
panic, 76
parenting
  as form of engineering, 24–5
  recipes for ideal, 67
parents, 23, 25, 64, 67
Pascal, Blaise, 62
Passage to India, A (E. M. Forster), 175–6
patience, 24, 131, 157
  see also attentiveness; impatience
Paul (apostle), 7, 113
perfectionism
  Aristotle on, 66, 70
  as cause of procrastination, 63, 64, 65, 66, 68, 189 n. 11
  definition of, 66
  destructive, 63
  illusory nature of, 65, 69, 70
  lifelessness of, 69
  reasons for, 67–8
  strategy for overcoming, 69–70
Pessoa, Fernando, 125, 128
Pew Research Center, 22–3
Phillips, Adam, 105, 139, 176
Pieper, Josef, 186 n. 3
Plato, 15, 94, 107, 180
play, spirit of
  comparison with cult of autonomy, 96

INDEX

play, spirit of (*cont.*)
    comparison with cult of work, 87–8, 96
    definition, 95
    etymology, 93–4
    exemplified in *Groundhog Day*, 88–90, 90, 91
    Friedrich Nietzsche on, 93
    and innovation, 96–8
    Johan Huizinga on, 94–6
    origin of human culture and, 94–6
    Plato on, 94
    purposiveness of, 92, 94, 99
    pursuit of life priorities in, 172
    Sigmund Freud on, 92–3
pleasure, 144
    see also bliss; happiness; joy
Pomodoro® Technique, 11
present moment, the, 54, 148–9
    attentiveness to, 152, 155–6, 157–9, 161–2, 173
    goal-directed focus on, 51, 149, 150–2
    Goethe on, 148, 149, 151
    Seneca on, 157–8, 161
    see also journey, the
pride, 68
priorities, *see* life priorities (goals)
privilege, inherited, 39, 56
procrastination
    and *acedia*, 106, 122, 124
    and *akrasia*, 108, 109
    Augustine and, 9–10
    as cause of boredom, 129, 131
    as cause of regret, 103, 104, 106
    causes of, *see* causes of procrastination
    comparison with *dolce far niente*, 7
    comparison with indolence, 6
    conventional solutions to, 10–11, 11–12, 43, 171
    distraction not principal cause of, 162–3
    historical explanations of, 14–18
    and importance of timing, 179–80
    liberation from, 181
    loss of sense of control due to, 93
    moral perspectives on, 15, 22
    origin of term, 22, 186 n. 1
    pertinacity of, 27
    reasons for, *see* causes of procrastination
    as result of feeling trapped, 128
    salutary aspects of, 174–7, 181
    seen as temporary, 10
    and self-sabotaged motivation, 6, 11
    short-term pleasure *v.* deferred harm at moment of, 107, 108

as stimulus to re-evaluate life priorities, 175
strategies for conquering, *see* strategies for conquering procrastination
use of regret by Søren Kierkegaard to overcome, 115
productivity, 41–2, 42
see also managerial-technocratic ethos; work
Proust, Marcel, 175
psychological sciences
explanations of procrastination in, 17–18, 139
see also Freud, Sigmund; Phillips, Adam

Ratelband, Émile, 35, 36
reason, 15
receptivity, 156, 157
see also attentiveness
recognition, 54–5, 56
cult of autonomy and need for, 57
liberation from excessive dependence on, 57–8, 61
posthumous, 58–61
see also esteem
Reformation, Protestant, 25, 28
see also Calvin, John; Luther, Martin
regret
and *akrasia*, 107, 109, 110
Aristotle on, 107, 109, 110, 192 n. 4

authenticity impelled by, 115
creative nature of, 106
and cult of autonomy, 103–4
and cult of work, 103–4
delayed nature of, 107
existential choices impelled by, 115
impact on Søren Kierkegaard of, 110–15
and life priorities, 103–4, 106, 107, 109, 110, 115, 172–3, 174, 178
as result of procrastination, 103, 104, 106
over unlived life, 104–5
remorse, 103, 107
restlessness, 17, 168, 186 n. 3
as precondition for distraction, 121, 122, 164
see also distraction
retirement, 8, 138
Rilke, Rainer Maria, 141
romantic relationships, 24, 63–4, 65, 92
Søren Kierkegaard and Regine Olsen, 110–14
see also marriage
Rousseau, Jean-Jacques, 57, 130
Russell, Bertrand, 49, 188 n. 9

sacredness, 28
Sagan, Carl, 62

211

INDEX

Sandel, Michael, 38, 39, 43, 188 n. 9
Sartre, Jean-Paul, 125
sati, 161
Schopenhauer, Arthur, 137–8, 149–50
scientific innovation, 96–8
self-determination, 34–5, 36, 38, 56
   see also autonomy
self-knowledge, 37
self-transcendence, 145
Seneca, 157–8, 161
Sennett, Richard, 69
senses, 144
Setiya, Kieran, 145
'seven deadly sins', 122
sexual orientation, 35
shame, 53, 103
sirens (*Odyssey*), 167
Slow Productivity (Cal Newport), 11
social media, 55, 57, 59, 163, 167, 168
   see also distraction: digital
Socrates, 107
Solomon, King, 180
sorrow, 15
Stendhal, 140–1
   syndrome, 141
Stoicism, 157, 158, 159, 161–2
   Seneca, 157–8, 161
strategies for conquering procrastination, 171–4
   affirming cosmic insignificance of humanity, 62
   attaining intimate awareness of death as ever-present possibility, 74, 172
   avoiding mirage of complete fulfilment, 173
   avoiding perfectionism, 65
   cultivating attentiveness, 152, 155–6, 161, 173
   embracing spirit of play, 99, 172
   importance of timing to, 181
   limiting dependence on recognition of others, 57–8
   lowering stakes of life priorities, 49–53, 62–3, 171–2
   making life choices informed by boredom, 129, 131, 172–3
   making life choices informed by regret, 110, 115, 172–3
students, 39, 64
substitute activities, *see* displacement activities
success
   fear of, 137–9, 140
   meritocratic view of, 38–9
   sabotage of own, 6
   undermined by questioning its value, 136
suffering, 161
   Arthur Schopenhauer on, 137, 138, 149
   Buddhist view of, 159
Suzuki, D. T., 149, 196 n. 23

Tangney, June P., 53
tedium, 128
  see also boredom
teenagers, 22
  see also children
Thomas Aquinas, 15, 122, 123–4
time
  nature of, 126–7, 127
  passing of, 53, 121, 126, 164
  and selfhood, 127
  wasting of, 26–7, 40
timing in life
  and cult of autonomy, 178
  Friedrich Nietzsche on, 179
  importance of, 178–81
  see also 'organizing idea'
    (Friedrich Nietzsche)
Tolstoy, Leo, 135, 136–7, 143–4, 145, 152
truth, relativity of, 35
Tyranny of Merit, The (Michael Sandel), 38

unconscious, 110
universe (cosmos)
  as child at play, 93
  indifference to humanity of, 61–2
  presence in the moment of, 159, 161
  rebellion against, 123
universities, 39
  see also colleges
unlived life, the 104–6

van Gogh, Vincent, 157
Vaucanson, Jacques de, 98

Vidal, Gore, 37–8
Virgil, 83
vocation, 35
  as displacement activity, 8–9
  distraction from pursuit of, 121, 122, 164
  increasing ability to change, 177–8
  perceived incompatibility with marriage, 112, 114, 115
  see also life priorities (goals)

Wallace, David Foster, 125, 131–2
Warren, James, 107
what-if/if-only life, 104–6
Wilson, A. N., 135
Wittgenstein, Ludwig, 69
Wonderland: How Play Made the Modern World (Steven Johnson), 96
work, 21–6, 28–30, 38, 40–1, 43–4, 155
  constraints on autonomy in, 37–8
  for its own sake, 186 n. 3
  'iron cage' metaphor for cult of, 40
  managerial-technocratic ethos of cult of, 42–3, 174
  managerialism and cult of, 24, 28–9
  moral perspectives on cult of, 25, 28, 38

work (*cont.*)
  opposition to cult of, 40, 41–3, 187 n. 9
  origin in Protestant Reformation of cult of, 25
  procrastination caused by cult of, 21–2, 29–30
  regret and cult of, 103–4
  as source of motivation, 21
  spirit of play compared with cult of, 87–8, 96
  Thomas Carlyle on cult of, 28
  see also career
work–life balance, 29, 40, 42
working week, length of, 29, 37, 41–3
Works and Days (Hesiod), 14

Yeats, W. B., 59
Young, Michael, 38

Zen Buddhism, 149